Acknowledgements

For their research and help I should like to thank my mother, Edith M. Pick, and my colleague Freda Steel. For their generous compilation of case study material I owe a particular debt to Paul Bassett of the Glasgow Citizen's Theatre, Charles Bishop, Caroline Gardiner and Steve Murphy of the Half Moon Theatre. David Brierley kindly sent me figures from the Royal Shakespeare Company, and I have elsewhere used figures from Rod Fisher and his colleagues at the Arts Council of Great Britain. Dr. Barry Smith sent me useful information on the amateur theatre, and my colleague Michael Quine was always on hand with helpful comments. All opinions and all errors are entirely mine.

J.P.

INTRODUCTION

Many business reports have only two tenses: immediate present and future conditional. The lack of interest in the history of an industry often means that those who work in it are not aware of how the past conditions the way they work today; whether these are particular obstacles like legal constraints, or more general things like cost structure or the "terms of trading". Sometimes executives in an industry will understand the past only through the distorting prism of the history of their own company. Comedia's *Media and Communications Industry Profile Series* therefore contains a short historical analysis designed to clarify how the past has contributed to the present.

In the course of our own consultancy work, we have been struck by the number of managers and executives – all efficient and successful – who know *what* is happening in their industry but do not really understand *why*. Often in these industries, people say "Oh, but we're different from other industries," and this refrain is used to obscure any discussion of why things happen in the particular way they do. One of the main purposes of our series is to get at the "operating dynamics"; to see what makes an industry tick, rather than just provide cautiously hedged predictions about the future. The reports, therefore, contain a section on the major issues of technology, markets and legislation.

There is also a section of case studies which look at management methods, merger and international takeovers of UK companies, and single industry firms going into multi-media developments. By looking at particular cases, the reports seek to identify changes affecting the industry as a whole.

Finally, the reports contain a section which looks at areas of growth; where new markets will develop and in which new technologies will be decisive in shaping the future.

This report follows a similar structure to the others published in the series, so that they provide a basis for comparison, where appropriate, between different industries.

At the end there is a full list of the other industries covered in the series.

Russell Southwood
Series Editor

Contents

POLITICAL ECONOMY

1.1. History of British theatre

THE BRITISH THEATRE HAS NEVER BEEN free of legal control, nor - except for a brief period in the late nineteenth century - has it been free of various forms of state fiscal control. Officialdom has always kept a wary eye upon an industry which has simultaneously the power to inspire the highest patriotism and to foment revolution.

Control of the theatre has varied from outright prohibition of all plays - in the Commonwealth, from 1642 to 1660 - to the subtler controls of licensing, state censorship, taxation and selective state subsidy. The evolution of the present theatre industry, which stretches from 1660 to the present day, is in general a piecemeal development of an industry which has neither been permitted to exist within an entirely free market economy, nor centrally planned. As a consequence the theatre is now subject to a variety of influences and controls, many of which have outlived their original objectives, and have no common aim nor purpose. It is thus difficult to explain *rationally* why it does things in the way that it does, and harder still to apply notions of managerial efficiency to it.

The first decisive act of state control came with the so-called Restoration of the Theatre in 1660. The term *restoration* is indeed a misnomer, for Charles I did not restore the theatre that the Puritans had dismantled earlier in the century. He permitted plays to be performed only in two London theatres, which held Royal Patents for the purpose. (Other theatres in the land could present supposedly harmless bills of music and dancing, but not the spoken drama, which thus came to be called *legitimate*.) That act remained in force for nearly two centuries, and although other cities in their turn were granted patent theatres (Norwich and Bath in 1768, Liverpool 1771, Manchester 1775, Bristol 1778 and Newcastle in 1788), it had a profound effect in separating the privileged urban audiences at the "Theatre Royals" from common theatregoers, and in the separation of "illegitimate" entertainment from "legitimate" theatre in government and public attitudes. In addition, the restored theatre of the late seventeenth century was utterly different in style from the popular theatre Shakespeare had known a century earlier. The buildings were roofed, and much smaller; the plays (now performed by actresses as well as actors) were in subject matter and performance of intimate interest only to London high society.

Legal control of theatre by government was greatly increased by the *Theatre Censorship Act*, introduced by Walpole in 1737. The act reintroduced the notion that anyone acting for gain, without licence from the Lord Chamberlain, should be deemed a rogue and vagabond, and, more significantly, ruled that no new plays nor additions to old plays might be acted until they had obtained the permission of the Lord Chamberlain. This act, which was effective in the British theatre until its eventual repeal in the 1960s, played a major part in the emasculation of the national drama. (The history of stage censorship in Britain is not brutal, rather one of replacing challenging drama with platitude, of an insidious softening of language and ideas, of a middle class cosiness substituted for the rougher attack of populist drama.) By the middle of the eighteenth century legitimacy and gentility were thus bound together.

The popular theatre - the "illegitimate" theatre of the non-patent city theatres, of the small towns, and of the barnstorming performances - grew throughout the eighteenth century in spite of its constraints. By the end of the century almost every town of more than about 750 inhabitants had its theatre, and more than half of the population must have gone two or three times a year to see some kind of theatrical performance. The theatres, and the tiny fit-up companies that toured fairgrounds, village barns and other makeshift venues, were wholly commercial in their internal management and in their general aims. They ran up against authority only when seeking a licence to erect a theatre building, when caught performing unlicensed material (in the early nineteenth century professional actors caught performing Shakespeare in non-patent theatres were prosecuted) or caught offending against the bye-laws which restrained the freedom of entertainers in many of the older boroughs.

Fashionable resorts such as Bath or Lichfield had several theatres, running seasons of the drama and attracting sufficient income not only to put their managers into profit, but to attract fashionable London performers in favoured roles. Unfashionable towns also had flourishing theatres. A small market town such as Retford in Nottinghamshire had a theatre, built in 1789, which could house almost half of the town's population of 1,034. It had a layered pricing structure (a practice which was almost universal until the 1970s) of 3s. for a box seat, 2s. for the pit and 1s. for the gallery. The top price was about half of the weekly income of the skilled labourer or small farmer, and even the lowest price more than the cost of a simple inn meal, but nevertheless the theatre ran profitably for more than fifty years. It was not until the nineteenth century that theatre-going became an essentially urban pleasure. A market town such as Retford was thus no worse served than an industrial conurbation such as Birmingham, which had in the eighteenth century twenty times the population of Retford, but had never more than three theatres, and for long periods only one.

Hardly anywhere outside London and the resort towns was it possible to make a reasonable living from running one theatre, or from running one company. Audiences, though proportionately much larger than in the twentieth century, were rarely sufficient for one theatre to cover production costs, and even in the metropolis managers had to aim to recover production costs in a handful of performances, and trust that some shows would draw the town

longer and so take them into profit. Outside London, therefore, the practice of running a circuit grew. In this way a production could "tour" a number of theatres in an area, thus extending its run, and limiting the proportion of the original production costs which had to be set against each performance. Many circuits were built up and controlled by shrewd managers who may thus be said to have created many of the elements of modern commercial management. Samuel Butler, for example, who built and opened six new houses on his Yorkshire circuit between 1787 and 1805, played a prominent part in the business and political life of the area, as did Fisher in East Anglia, who built 11 new theatres on his circuit in 20 years. The theatre manager thus became a respected local figure, although the work he was promoting was sometimes "illegitimate" in government eyes. Some managers, however, built successful businesses and good local reputations upon the provincial patent theatres, notably Mrs. Baker in Canterbury and James Whitley of Chester. Most famous of all was Tate Wilkinson, who ran the circuit based on the twin patent theatres of York and Hull and who, although he had relinquished management of the Hull theatre in 1814, was still being referred to respectfully in the local prints as "The Late Manager" in 1820.

In towns without a patent theatre, and in suburbs at some distance from the centralised legitimate houses, there was a growing call to repeal the 1660 *Patent Theatres Act*. This was compounded by the rapid growth in the early nineteenth century of the new industrial towns, which found themselves without a "Theatre Royal" and thus cut off from the legitimate drama. Accordingly, in 1843, one of the main functions of the *Theatres Act* was to render it legal for any properly licensed theatre to present the legitimate drama. In some provincial cities new theatres were quickly built. Birmingham, for example, whose population rapidly expanded to some 250,000 by the middle of the century, licensed a stream of new theatres shortly afterwards; the Operetta House, Day's Crystal Palace (later the Empire) and the Amphitheatre, in a single year, 1862. They were joined

THEATRE, RETFORD.

LAST NIGHT THIS SEASON.

FOR THE BENEFIT OF

MR. MANLY.

On SATURDAY Evening, August the 27th, 1825,

Will be Acted the popular Play of THE

HYPOCRITE.

It is a consideration of a truly melancholy nature to look around in this empire, and behold so vast a portion of the lower classes of society gradually renouncing the charities and ethics of Christianity, to embrace opinions which are not only hostile to the main ends of our holy religion, but utterly irreconcileable to the reasoning faculties of the mind; and, in pursuance of this inexplicability, thousands of miserable zealots ponder in thought upon points that are entirely irrational, until the brain becomes diseased, and then sink from dispair to madness, into a dark and comfortless grave, where hope hath no influence! All those who are attached in heart and spirit to the furtherance of the doctrines of the Established Church of this country, should lend their aid in support of every endeavour (whether theatrically expressed, or otherwise,) that leads to the destruction of those pernicious errors of opinion, which tend so woefully to undermine and overthrow the fair order of worship, and upraise that hideous monster, FANATICISM, upon the ashes of reason and true faith.

Cantwell, Mr. MANLY
Sir John Lambert, Mr. FROMOW—Col. Lambert, Mr. FREER
Darnley, Mr. PINDAR—Seyward, Mr. WARREN—Mawworm, Mr. CARROL

Old Lady Lambert, Mrs. SIDNEY—Charlotte, Mrs. MANLY
Young Lady Lambert, Miss FRASER——Betty, Mrs. GARDINER

A COMIC SONG, BY MR. CARROL.
A SONG BY MR. HOOPER.
A Comic Song, by Mr. Fromow.

After which will be presented (never acted here,) an entire new Melo Dramatic and novel Entertainment, with new Scenery, Music, and appropriate Decorations, entitled THE

Floating Beacon;

OR, THE NORWEGIAN WRECKERS.

Angerstoff, (Captain of the Beacon) Mr. FREER
Maurice, } his Companions, { Mr. GARDINER
Ormoloff, } { Mr. PALMER
Wergnstadt, (an old Fisherman) Mr. FROMOW
Frederick, (a supposed Orphan) Mr. WARREN—Junk, (a British Sailor) Mr. CARROL
Sailors, Marines, &c.

Mariette, (the Woman of the Beacon) Mrs. MANLY
Christine, (Wergnstadt's Daughter) Miss CHERRY

This piece is founded on a well known account given in the Edinburgh Magazine, under the Title of " THE FLOATING BEACON," and another entitled, " THE FLORIDA PILOT." The Plot is carried on on Board the

NORWAY LIGHT VESSEL;

To represent which, the whole of the Stage is converted into the

MAIN DECK,

Where the scene of action is principally developed, and from its remoteness from all other communication, the

VESSEL IS SUPPOSED TO BE THE SCENE OF

Many Atrocities, and even Murders!

The novelty of the action being carried on, and conveying the imagination into the midst of the Ocean, for the portraiture of a very interesting Drama has made it so attractive in the Metropolis, that it has already been acted nearly 200 Nights.

BOXES, 3s. PIT, 2s. GAL. 1s. Tickets and Places for the Boxes to be had of Mr. Dewhirst.
Also, of MR. MANLY, at MR. BAILEY's, Bridge Gate.
Doors to be opened at Six, and the Curtain to rise at Seven o'Clock.
All demands on the Theatre are requested to be sent in on Saturday, the 27th inst. by 12 o'Clock.

Dewhirst, Printer, Retford.

by Coutts' Theatre (1868), the Steam Clock (1879), The Grand (1893) and the Theatre Royal, Aston (1896) which, together with the surviving patent theatre, the Royal, meant that the new industrial city had an impressive commercial theatre life to set alongside its other civic amenities.

The smaller country theatres, and with them the country circuits, disappeared in the nineteenth century, and theatrical life tended to be increasingly concentrated in the larger cities. This was in part because of the growth of cheap transport, particularly the local railways, and partly because of the growth of widespread press advertising. The country dweller and the inhabitants of the market towns were less frequently visited by professional players, but were encouraged instead to visit the "theatreland" of Manchester, Leeds or Birmingham and, of course, of the capital itself.

In London there was no spate of theatre building immediately following the 1843 act. The most immediate effect was that legitimate theatre companies established themselves in the suburbs. Such companies as Samuel Phelps' Sadler's Wells company, and the Shakespearean players at the Brittania, Hoxton, were able to attract large audiences and to make classical drama a commercial proposition well away from the newly emergent "West End". For a time, the divisions between the privileged "legitimate" theatre and the popular "illegitimate" theatre lessened, and the theatre as a whole may be said to have passed into popular control. However, in the 1860s, there was a move towards establishing a new kind of exclusive enclave in London, and this was ultimately to redivide the theatre industry.

This may properly be dated from the Bancrofts' management of the theatre which they re-named the Prince of Wales's, and which in 1865 established itself as the most fashionable in London. At this theatre (and, later, during their short but lucrative management of the Theatre Royal in the Haymarket) the Bancrofts presented a new kind of production, "Cup and Saucer Comedy", which was to set the style of what has been for more than a century the

typical "West End success". With it, they established a new kind of theatre management, which aimed to play to the well-to-do, and which had an entirely different kind of financial logic from all that had gone before.

The new kind of "West End" theatre depended upon presentation in a small but well appointed theatre, in which the pit had given way to stalls, and in which the stalls and dress circle represented the majority of the management income. Thus the huge theatres presenting the legitimate drama at the time of the 1843 Act, holding some 3,000 who paid small sums, were replaced by the Prince of Wales's and its successors, holding a few hundred, paying 7s. 6d. or, later, 10s. for the better seats. The productions mounted by the Bancrofts and their followers still had high production costs (scenery and appointments were of good standard), but the audience was teased out over much longer runs and, as much smaller casts meant that running costs were low, the profit was very large. Indeed, after a total of 20 years' management, the Bancrofts were able to retire with profits from theatre management of more than £180,000.

By the end of the nineteenth century the "West End" London theatre consisted of small and fashionable houses playing decorous dramas to ever-longer runs. An ever-higher proportion of the income came from the expensive seats (between 60 and 70 per cent in most theatres came from stalls and dress circle), and the newly-introduced publicity formats and booking schemes were targeted on high-income groups. There was thus extensive theatre advertising in the high class *Daily Telegraph*, but none in the popular *Police Gazette*. The booking offices in the West End closed well before working people could get to them after a day's work and, in some cases, they required that would-be theatre goers were dressed formally to book seats, similarly attired as would be necessary for them to be allowed in to stalls or dress circle of a West End theatre. The pattern of long runs in the West End suggests the increasing affluence of London managers in the last years of the century.

Although the suburban and provincial theatre aped the West End on stage, it did not attempt to emulate the small theatre/long run theatre economy. The theatres built in the suburbs of London and the larger cities, and the theatres in provincial cities, were still typically of 2,000–2,500 capacity, with lower admission charges (1s. to 4s. 6d. would still be a typical provincial theatre price range). They tended to be grouped in national or regional circuits, after the manner of the smaller eighteenth century circuits, relying not on long runs, but on long *tours*, to be profitable. By the turn of the century the industry had reached a position of maxi-mum exploitation of a production; it would run for as long as possible in London, drawing the maximum profit from a long West End presentation, and would then tour the larger provincial theatres "direct from the West End", sometimes for several years. The managers of the provincial theatres would agree a "split" with the London production company, to their mutual profit. Here, for example, are the figures of Henry Irving's Lyceum Company's visit to the Royalty Theatre, Glasgow. As will be seen, the profit to the host theatre and to the visiting company are remarkably even:

WEST END "RUNS" IN THE NINETEENTH CENTURY

	Over 100 Perfs	Over 200 Perfs	Over 300 Perfs
1840s	5	1	0
1850s	16	0	0
1860s	52	11	6
1870s	107	25	9
1880s	157	46	22
1890s	169	58	24

ACCOUNTS FOR THE ROYALTY THEATRE, GLASGOW, WEEK ENDING 5th NOVEMBER, 1881

	£	s	d
RECEIPTS	2,089	1	6
EXPENDITURE			
Salaries	498	6	0
Printing	17	2	0
Advertising	93	4	10
Cost of supernumeraries (Extras)	13	6	0
Sundries	58	13	1
Share to Royalty (⅓ of receipts)	696	7	2
PROFIT TO LYCEUM COMPANY	**712**	**2**	**5**

In the early years of the twentieth century a number of large managements (notably the organisations of Moss and of Oswald Stoll) came to control chains of London and provincial theatres and thus exercised an oligarchic control over the commercial British theatre.

However, the apparent commercial freedom in which the Bancrofts, Irving and their immediate successors flourished was short-lived. The theatre buildings were increasingly subject, during the nineteenth century, to building and licensing controls – and although managers fretted about the number of exits they were forced to build, light and man, or about the expensive new regulations over stage lighting, or the erection of crush barriers and safety doors, they had no choice but to comply. Being licensed to manage a theatre was no longer easy to achieve; after the *London Theatres Building Act*

of 1879 more than a third of the capital's Music Halls were refused a licence, and one consequence of the increasing building regulations was that running costs for theatres grew rapidly. It became much more expensive to instal and operate scenery and lighting that complied with the increasingly stringent regulations, while the larger number of exits required, coupled with the increased need for proper safety supervision, meant that front-of-house running costs also increased. The theatre industry's economy had, by the end of the nineteenth century, radically changed from Shakespeare's day, where income was divided up between the players and playwright, actor, technician and administrator were all one man. Analysis of the total costs of Irving's Lyceum management shows that only about a third of the total expenditure of professional theatre is now on the performers.

SUMMARY OF EXPENDITURE
Henry Irving's Lyceum Management 1879 – 1899

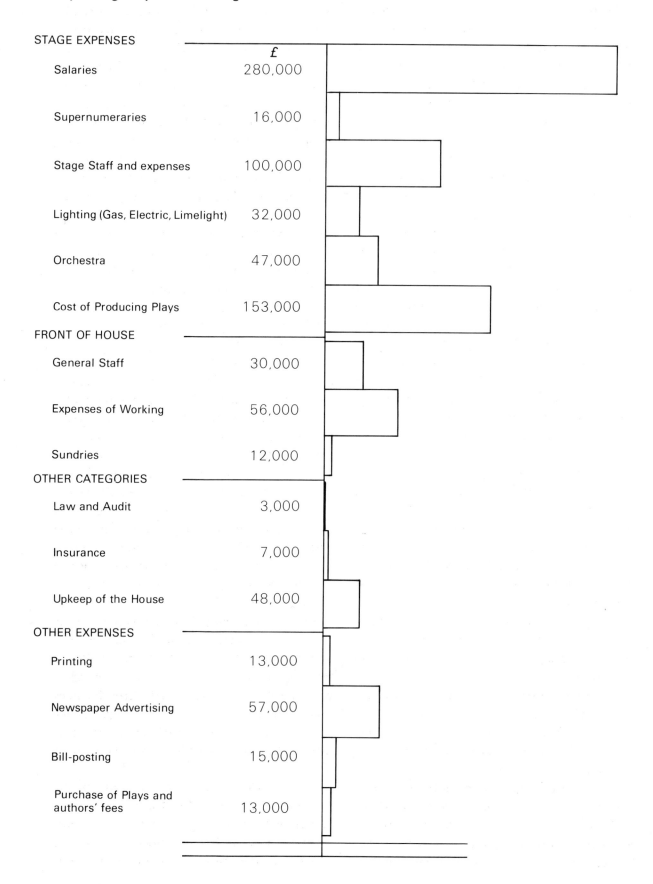

	£
STAGE EXPENSES	
Salaries	280,000
Supernumeraries	16,000
Stage Staff and expenses	100,000
Lighting (Gas, Electric, Limelight)	32,000
Orchestra	47,000
Cost of Producing Plays	153,000
FRONT OF HOUSE	
General Staff	30,000
Expenses of Working	56,000
Sundries	12,000
OTHER CATEGORIES	
Law and Audit	3,000
Insurance	7,000
Upkeep of the House	48,000
OTHER EXPENSES	
Printing	13,000
Newspaper Advertising	57,000
Bill-posting	15,000
Purchase of Plays and authors' fees	13,000

20th Century

In the first half of the twentieth century there were three general developments in theatre economy which, all for different reasons, seemed to make the industry less open and, so far as the term may be used, less efficient. The first was the growing concentration of power within a relatively small group of theatre owners and producers, who worked largely for their own advantage and profit, and sometimes tried to exclude competition by what would now be regarded as unfair trading practices. Essentially, the control of theatre lay in the interlocking empires of the West End. (Most number one and number two theatres in the land were playing productions "prior to" or "following" West End presentation, and most amateur societies were faithfully reproducing "West End successes". Control was formalised in the formation of the Society of West End Theatre Managers, a powerful group of major West End interests that had divided itself from the countrywide Theatrical Managers Association in 1908. The association, controlled to a large degree what was seen on our stages from Exeter to Aberdeen. By an incestuous process of subletting raised theatre rentals to a height which forbade outsiders from entering their charmed circle, they promoted their own style of drama and their own notions of "West End" stars. Through an unwritten oligarchy they controlled the theatre economy so that an ever-diminishing proportion of expenditure was on performers, and ever more spent on their own companies and the myriad advisers, consultants and experts that fronted them. Soon only about a fifth of the money which the public paid at the door was going to the performers whom they paid to see.

The second development was the growing power of the theatre backers, or "angels". Increased production costs were to a degree self-induced. The theatre is one of the few industries in which increased mechanisation has led to increased manning, and one of the few industries in which the administrative, technical and advisory staffs have grown steadily in contrast to the actual performers of the industrial task. The increase in costs seems to have led inexorably to

a need for greater capital investment at the start of each new production. However, the increased standardisation of the West End industry also meant that investment in a new production by a major concern was less risky than might have been thought. Fortunes were certainly lost by backers, sometimes because they interfered too much in the casting and presentation of the plays they supported. But a large number of people made a great deal of money by investing in safe, well-heeled West End productions which after a few weeks would "break even" on the original investment and would thereafter show a steady profit for the investor. The effect of this was partly to distort questions of real value (a second-rate actor or actress who was a favourite with the backers would be cast in preference to a better performer) but, more importantly, to standardise further the West End play and its production and presentation into a kind of stylish mediocrity.

The third distortion of the theatre economy was no fault of the West End managers. It was the introduction, in 1916, of an Entertainments Tax upon theatre tickets. This tax, supposedly introduced only for the duration of the war, lasted for 40 years, and not only raised the costs of theatre presentation in general, but in particular disproportionately raised the price of cheaper theatre seats. This further discouraged theatre-going among the poorer sections of the cities. They turned in ever-increasing numbers to the cheaper, more comfortable cinemas which were springing up in every town and suburb in which theatres had stood 50 years before. Indeed, many theatres became cinemas between the wars – including such famous houses as the Royal Court Theatre in Sloane Square. This taxation thus reintroduced a measure of indirect control of theatre economics (which the 1843 *Theatres Act* had partly removed) which was added to the control the state had – through censorship – over the product itself.

Nevertheless, until the outbreak of the second World War, the British theatre ran almost entirely without subsidy, and almost entirely in profit. This included not only the West End, the touring theatres and the suburban theatres of the larger cities, but the growing number of repertory theatres also. The repertory movement in Britain began with Miss Horniman's opening of the Gaiety theatre in Manchester in 1908. Thereafter, a growing number of theatres were opened in Britain in which a permanent company played a series of different plays which ran for a week, or occasionally a fortnight, and built up a devoted following in their area for what was often a surprisingly adventurous programme. Alfred Waring founded a rep in Glasgow in 1910, and Basil Dean opened the Liverpool Playhouse on similar lines in 1911. He was succeeded there by William Armstrong, who was director from 1922 to 1944 and under whose guidance the rep was in continuous profit. Expenses never exceeded £500 a week and they made money on everything, "even Shakespeare".

Most reps started life on a shoestring, but an exception was the Birmingham rep, opened in 1913 by Barry Jackson; that theatre is reputed to have cost him, as patron, in excess of £100,000 during his lifetime. Others, however, sprang up between the wars without such patronage – and there were reps between the wars in Nottingham, Glasgow, Oxford, Chesterfield, Ipswich, Salisbury, Leatherhead, Hull and Cambridge and many other towns. Their programmes were ambitious – Sheffield offered an entire *season* of European drama – and they formed an informal association of repertory theatres, exchanging information on management and production techniques. There were more than 40 by 1939, all with high ambitions, but running commercially and without state aid.

Immediately after the war there was a boom in repertory, and for a few years almost every town of any size had a "rep". By the late 40s, when the only competition was the cinema (in 1949 on average every adult in Britain went to the cinema once a week) and drama on radio ("Saturday Night Theatre" on the radio was heard each week by a third of the entire adult population), there were more than 400 reps running in Britain. Most were commercial, and aimed to be profitable, but their time was short. Increasingly, following Bristol's lead, the major

provincial reps turned to the cushion of state subsidy. In the 50s, more than 200 commercial theatres closed and the prevailing belief was that repertory could only be saved by the companies being charitable in aim, non-profit-making in nature, and coming to rely upon the state annually making good the gap between their costs and the income from the box office. From the start grants were seen as synonymous with quality, and the size of grant given to Bristol, or Nottingham, was seen not as a mark of bad housekeeping, but as a symbol of quality, guaranteed by the new Arts Council of Great Britain.

1.2. Subsidy and its effects

The notion of state subsidy for the theatre – inevitably bound up with the century-long argument over the desirability or otherwise of a "National" theatre – had for a century or more been resisted by theatre businessmen. The idealists argued that state subsidy would give a degree of security to the acting profession, it would be an agency for the moral improvement of society, or create a stimulating centre of prestige work which would be the envy of the world – all arguments offered at the end of the nineteenth century. The men at the heart of the theatre business usually retorted that government bureaucrats, who didn't understand the mysterious nature of professional theatre, would inevitably take over, and that a subsidised theatre would, in the words of Henry Peat (1879) be staffed by actors well past their prime playing to a well-heeled audience too polite or too inept to notice the *senile incapacity* of the whole organisation. In any case, it was felt that Irving at the Lyceum, and, later, Tree at His Majesty's, had already created everything a major national theatre should be – ensemble playing of the classics at a high standard, the best in design and production, a high degree of security for the best artistes, and even (through Tree's formation of R.A.D.A.) professional training.

There was never any noticeable change of heart within the profession, and a state subsidy system was created obliquely, by a series of particular circumstances, rather than by any change in managerial will, or as a result of any thorough-going survey of theatre finances and managerial practices. During the Second World War, following the formation of the Committee (later the Council) for the Encouragement of Music and the Arts (CEMA), a series of decisions were taken – for little reason other than in response to immediate wartime pressures – which effectively set the parameters of the subsidy system operating in the contemporary theatre, and may be said, therefore, to be at the root of many of the tensions and muddles in modern theatre management.

It is important to recall that at the outbreak of war a second, much larger, organisation had been formed, largely to bring a wide spectrum of the performing arts to the troops and wartime workers; this was the Entertainments National Services Association (ENSA), which was heavily subsidised by government, and 12 times larger than CEMA. CEMA was set up by a grant from the U.S. Pilgrim Trust, and began as an organisation devoted to helping *amateurs*. Its first accounts show large numbers of small grants to enable amateur dramatic societies and amateur choral societies to continue working in wartime. However, in 1940, following a *Times* leader (which, as so often, summarised a discussion which had occurred amongst the great and the good, rather than stimulated one) suggesting that our finest artists were being neglected by the populist activities of ENSA, CEMA abruptly changed course, announced it was to be concerned with the finest things done by *professional* artists, and thereafter acted and pronounced in such a way as to erode the distinction between the *best* art and *state subsidised* art.

In the theatre CEMA acted in two ways. First, it began to subsidise its own professional tours, largely of theatrical classics, and in its publicity began to abrogate ENSA's right to having any wider social purpose – *their* plays were entertainment, CEMA's were art and were self-evidently improving the quality of life. Second, and more importantly, it moved to give subsidy to established theatre companies which were playing classical and hence improving works. The first production subsidised, by a guarantee against it losing money when it

played in London, was John Gielgud's production of *Macbeth*, presented on tour by H. M. Tennent Ltd.

There was a difficulty here. H. M. Tennent had grown to be the most influential and, in most respects the largest, of the commercial organisations operating within the West End theatre. It was plainly a money-making, private enterprise. CEMA could not, by its constitution, give grants to an organisation not recognised as a charity, which operated on a profit-making basis, and was not a company limited by guarantee. To accommodate this, Tennents created a second, parallel company, Tennent Productions Ltd., which put on the same productions but which, by a series of accounting devices, was properly constituted as a separate organisation of purely charitable intent, seeking to educate and improve the quality of London life with the selfsame production of *Macbeth* which, in the provinces, had set out to make a profit.

For its part, CEMA gave aid in the form of a Guarantee Against Loss, which meant that accounts had to be drawn up and the loss properly accounted, before the deficit would be paid off by CEMA. This was the kind of practice adopted for many years by CEMA's successor, the post-war Arts Council, until it became clear that having to wait for a year and more before payment meant companies promised large grants could no longer afford to pay for the debts which mounted annually. The Arts Council then began the practice of paying quarterly and then, to the larger companies, monthly, a proportion of the promised guarantee against loss.

It will thus be obvious that the practice, begun in 1943 by CEMA, of paying grant aid to charitable companies in this form led to their clients and those of the later constituted Arts Council adopting a form of *deficit budgeting* which meant that in their expenditure on productions, in their staffing, and in their seat pricing, theatre organisations *aimed to make* the promised loss. This habit became so ingrained within theatre outside the West End that in the 70s and 80s taking an enormous state grant for theatre work came to be called "breaking even". The National Theatre, for example, announced in 1984 that it required an additional £1½ million in public subsidy in addition to the £6½ million it annually receives from the Arts Council, and the £¾ million it receives from the Greater London Council. As evidence of its good housekeeping it announced to the world that it had "broken even" between 1979 and 1983 – whereas if its accounts are looked at in ordinary accountancy terms it actually *lost* £10 million between 1979 and 1981 and nearly half as much again during the following two years; all sums paid to it by the Arts Council and the GLC as *guarantees against loss*.

There have, however, been significant shifts in Arts Council thinking over the *nature* of state subsidy between the early days of CEMA and its present managerial activities. Ostensibly the stance has not changed. Panels of disinterested experts advise the Council's officers; they look at both the artistic and financial realms of each prospective theatrical "client", and, in cooperation with the client organisation, agree on a proper annual grant – to be paid as a loss guarantee. All clients are (as they must be by the charter of the Council) charitable companies and (as they have no need to be, by constraint of the charter or for any other reason) professional. But the real nature of state subsidy has markedly changed, and with it the impact of subsidy upon the political economy of the theatre. Looking at the period following the 1945 creation of the Arts Council, it is possible to discern four phases.

Post War Reconstruction 1945-50

In its earliest years neither the Arts Council nor its clients saw their work as other than temporary. "I do not think," said J. B. Priestley in 1947, "that we shall require subsidy for very long." Laurence Olivier, writing in the same year, saw it as encouraging that a number of theatre organisations had not needed to take up their guarantee against loss. The Council saw itself as a reactive organisation, helping where asked with post-war reconstruction of the arts industry. In economic terms it saw itself as having the power sometimes to act as a corrective, when market forces, temporarily distorted by the lasting effects of the war, were seen to be working against the long-term interests of the best art. (The exception was the Royal Opera House which from the first was seen as having a long-term dependancy upon the new Council.)

Selective Development 1950-65

By 1950 the annual government grant to the Arts Council as a whole had grown from £175,000 in 1945 to £500,000. The Council now saw itself as a permanent feature of British life but, because of the relatively puny size of its resources, able only to make selective intrusions in the arts markets. Such intrusions were, however, seen not as a short-term shoring up of an industrial weakness, but as an integral part of favoured clients' industrial development. Theatre companies favoured with grants were characterised not as weak and fallible (and thus in need of state charity) but the "best". The *symbolic* value of receiving state aid – it proved you were serious, worthwhile art – thus came to be great; none of the old stigma of relying on government aid attached to arts subsidy. Coupled with this there was a noticeable desire on the part of the Council to stay small, to nourish a small and manageable elite of theatres (as well as galleries and orchestras) which would be – to use a phrase subsequently peddled by every Arts Council chairman – a jewel in the national crown. In 1956, stretching their imaginations as far as they could allow them to go, the Council said that £2½ million would adequately finance not only all the arts organisations judged to be in need of such patronage but would provide the money needed for the long-term rehousing of the arts.

Arts as Welfare 1965-1979

That increasingly narrow notion of the "arts" was challenged in the mid-60s by the publication of Jennie Lee's Paper *A Policy for the Arts*. This sought to establish a less narrow view within the Arts Council of what comprised the contemporary arts, and began to assert the notion that the width of the arts should somehow be accessible to all, a right rather than a privilege. The paper was, however, compounded of pieties about objectives but deficient on details about what could be done. Although the

Arts Council was not directly instructed to alter course - it was still common to assert that government would always remain at "arm's length" from artistic affairs - indirect pressures moved the Council to take account of new movements within the arts world. In the theatre the mid-60s saw the beginnings of "alternative" theatre groups, relying to a large degree upon subsidy for their survival, and of "community" theatre, where amateur artistic activity was motivated and led by state subsidised animateurs and state subsidised community groups. The fashionable language used by this newly-subsidised realm - they were "committed", doing "relevant" work, "reaching out" to the "community" - was aped by some of the more traditional repertory theatres, which suddenly saw merit (listening to the newly-adopted jargon in Arts Council circles) in holding "workshops", running Theatre In Education troupes that "reached out" amongst the young, and in putting an occasional "committed" play at a point in the season when the inevitable box office drop would do least harm.

The Arts Council usually attempted in its public pronouncements to say that it saw no long-term conflict between "community" and "high" art, and no essential divergence of interest between the new alternative theatre and the established one. Such edicts were, however, somewhat disingenuous - apart from anything else, sections of the alternative theatre pronounced as one of their objectives the destruction of establishment theatre activities - and relied upon steadily increasing state funding to stop radically-different kinds of organisations coming into direct conflict over resources. The Council was, in fact, funding theatrical organisations for totally different purposes - on the one hand to sustain a traditional repertoire of the classic national drama, and at the other extreme to enable a new class of people to participate in its destruction and replacement by new kinds of theatrical activity. As the Welfare period drew to its close, the tensions shown up by declining resources, the *Redcliffe Maud Report on Arts Funding in England and Wales* (1976) recommended that the function of developing arts as a part of general welfare be taken over by the Local Authorities.

Monetarist Planning 1979-1985

In the late 70s the Council departed from its previous ground. It adopted for the first time a central planning function - it created policies which it pronounced not as internal Arts Council strategies, but national plans. Second, and not without considerable internal strain, it was forced *de facto* to accept that the government in essence was no longer at arm's length from it, but that the Arts Council was in all important aspects a government bureaucracy. The two developments were inextricably intertwined. Thus, when a government report on the Royal Shakespeare Company, commissioned by an Arts Minister, said that the company should have an increase in its annual grant, the "marked" money was simply passed to the Arts Council for processing, and the Council's supposed independence of judgement counted for nothing. Attempting to react to its changed circumstances, and to demonstrate its own abilities as a kind of national management for the arts, the Council produced in 1984 a hastily-compiled "Strategy" for the decade 1984 - 1994, bizarrely entitled *The Glory of the Garden*. This bravely announced - confusing devolution with decentralisation - that power and money was to be "passed to" the regions. Whatever the intent may have been, before the close of 1984, the "strategy" was in ruins.

This was in part because of the profoundly disturbing effect in the arts economy of the government's intention to abolish the GLC and the Metropolitan Counties. The Counties had between them given arts subsidies in excess of £30 million annually, and the effect in London (where the GLC had given more than £20 million to the arts) was compounded by the fact that the GLC owned the South Bank site and there seemed no alternative to letting the Arts Council now run it. It was also because successive Arts Ministers in the new government were plainly committed to a new kind of monetarist policy in the arts industry. Large prestigious organisations with an international profile were deemed to be good for the economy (attracting tourists, raising Britain's prestige abroad, generating exports of art works) and -

providing they were run on sound business lines – were to be properly capitalised. For the rest, and leavened only by some mistily conceived "centres of excellence" in various key provincial towns, they were to be moved into a more commercial posture. They were to end the habits of deficit budgeting, seek to make themselves commercially viable and also seek commercial sponsorship.

Such conflicting pressures have left the Arts Council in a curious position, seeking to "plan" for an arts industry over which they have, in any case, only a partial control, and finding those plans in conflict with the directly monetarist ambitions of government. Thus, in 1984, the Council is forced to plan the running of the South Bank complex (from 1985), is forced to pass on greatly increased funding to one of its two major theatrical clients, and is being forcefully asked for a similar increase in its funding of the other. Meanwhile, it has to tell even such a prestigious provincial client as the Royal Exchange Theatre in Manchester that it must move towards an end to its practices of deficit budgeting, and that it will not get the extra money that it expected, as one of the promised beneficiaries of the "strategy" for the 80s. Once more, as in the early 70s, only greatly increased government funding of the Arts Council can paper over the chasms between its conflicting intentions towards the theatre.

Now, in the mid-80s, the British theatre consists of the "big two", the National and the RSC, and in London of the (largely unsubsidised) West End theatre – a complex of production companies and theatre owners that accounts usually for some 35 – 40 active theatres. There are some 35 provincial theatres, containing what are still called Repertory Companies for at least a part of the year, and some 15 substantial provincial theatres, without permanent companies, but able to take in a mixture of commercial productions, together with subsidised opera, dance and theatre (plus, in many cases, a major production by the local Operatic Society, which usually draws a paying audience larger than that attracted by professional work). Such theatres usually have a strong degree of support from their local authorities, and will often have carried out improvements with the aid of the Arts Council-administered "Housing the Arts" fund. There are some 35 government subsidised Touring Companies, many of them working in small venues (about another 25 have subsidy from other sources, including the Regional Arts Associations), while a further 45 small companies survive on short-term project grants, with short-term aid from particular councils and regional organisations that pay them for a week or a fortnight's work. Finally, there are some 750 smaller civic theatres and venues.

In terms of sheer quantity, the professional theatre is less active and occupied than the amateur. On a fully-active evening in the professional theatre less than one in five of all trained actors is likely to be employed, and the total number of professional productions – about 200 – is less than the number of amateur productions – about 500 – according to the Central Council for Amateur Theatres' 1980 figures. The difference would be much greater if all those amateur productions mounted by educational establishments were added to the equation. Even so, the difference is startling. It is not even true that there is a vast difference in the size of the respective average audiences. If one compares attendances at the repertory companies – as being midway between the small audiences of the fringe and alternative groups and the big audiences of the major West End theatres – with attendances at amateur shows, the difference is not as great as one might imagine. The repertory audiences currently average around 295; the last survey of amateur theatre audiences suggested that, on average, 537 people saw each amateur show and that the average audience per performance (often in very small venues) was 146. In Britain there are (excluding schools, colleges and universities) about 8,500 amateur drama societies, in contrast with the 350 or so professional production companies that may be said to be independently active in the course of any one year.

It would not, of course, be true to say that the amateur theatre does not enjoy any subsidy. It does. In the CCAT survey, around half of all societies in Britain said that they were receiving financial aid or that facilities were provided by their local authorities, free or at reduced charge. (Retford, whose eighteenth century professional theatre was discussed above, has an excellent theatre built for it by its local council.) In Figure 2, the subsidy is merged within the general costs of space in which to rehearse and perform; that figure would be much higher if there were no "hidden" subsidy. Subsidy does not show as a separate item for a second reason; few amateur groups gain "project" funding from local authorities or from regional arts associations.

AMATEUR THEATRE IN BRITAIN
Annual Income and Expenditure

Box Office
Receipts
and other
Earned Income.

Cost of rehearsal
Premises.
9.29%

Cost of premises
for performance.
23.83%

Production and
Stage Costs.
66.88%

Income

Expenditure

Inevitably, the present financial position of professional subsidised theatres is very much more complicated. The mere fact of having a wage bill at all compounds running costs in a theatre – for not only are agreed rates of pay for actors, technicians, musicians and other personnel continually rising, the cost of administrative time to compile salaries correctly rises alarmingly. A theatre employs people on many different kinds of union agreements, at unsocial hours at high rates, and demands of them unusual and complicated tasks for which rates must be agreed. The accounts of an amateur theatre are attractively simple but, although there are good managerial reasons for simplifying many of the financial practices that have grown with the years in professional theatre, it can never become as beguilingly simple as the amateur one so long as employment law remains as complex as it does.

The present effects of subsidy upon the professional theatre in Britain prompt several comments. The first is that there is intrinsically nothing in theatre which makes it inevitable that subsidy should account for about a half of a theatrical company's total income. This can be proved simply by looking at other Western countries' theatrical economies; in the US., the state subsidy accounts for less than 5%, in West Germany it is nearly 90%. We have come to think that it is "right" for subsidy to be about a half of total income because, over time, and by operating our own system of deficit budgeting, we have organised it like that. It could have been otherwise and, even now, if we make changes over time, it can be organised quite differently.

The second observation is that, whatever else it has done, the British subsidy system has certainly increased the number of apparently unproductive bureaucrats employed in the system. When the taxpayers' money has passed, at whatever cost, through the government bureaucracy, it then goes to the Arts Council whose deliberations over its ultimate destination remove a further 4 – 5% in administrative

ROYAL SHAKESPEARE COMPANY 1983/4
Summary of Income and Expenditure (Total Costs £10,783,763)

T.V., Films, Foreign Tours 2.70%
Sponsorship 2.36%

Grants
43.75%

Reduction of Accumulated
Deficit .45%

Box Office and
Other Earned
Income
51.64%

Income

Publicity 3.87%

Administration
5.35%

Workshops
9.04%

Cost of UK Touring
8.48%

Production Materials
7.36%

Salaries of all
artists – actors,
directors,
designers, etc.
29.71%

Cost of maintaining
Theatre buildings
36.19%

Expenditure

costs. It is then quite likely to be passed on to another bureaucratic layer – a regional arts association, say – which may well subtract another 15% for its own administrative expenses. When it arrives (in the form of promised guarantee against loss) it faces a much larger cut, for the complexities, real and induced, within modern theatre organisations always mean that a far lower percentage of income actually goes into the performers' pockets. In Shakespeare's day the actors got around 90% of the expenditure; by Irving's day (see Figure 1) it was around 33%; as the following table of income and expenditure for the Royal Shakespeare Company shows, the wage bill for *all* artists – musicians, designers, directors included – is usually less than 30% of total expenditure.

Such a dramatic change gives the lie to two often-repeated pieces of theatrical administration lore. First, the crucial difference between amateur and professional theatre does not lie in the fact that professional companies pay their performers; it lies in the vast bill *for offstage staff.* Second, it is sometimes argued that theatre costs must inevitably rise because the theatre is a labour intensive industry. There's no way, it is said, in which you can stage *Hamlet* with fewer actors so, in a mechanical age, the theatre cannot get any of the benefits of mechanisation and reduce its workforce, hence it must always suffer compounded inflation. The figures do not bear this out. As a matter of plain fact, both the National and Royal Shakespeare Companies use far fewer musicians and fewer actors in a contemporary production of *Hamlet* than did Henry Irving – while in newly mechanised areas such as sound control they employ far *more* people.

It is difficult to say how much of this is due to the "cushion" provided by state subsidy. The process of adding offstage staff (who work with rather more security in some cases than do playwrights or actors) has taken place gradually over a number of years. But it has occurred most strikingly in subsidised companies as a comparison of staffing in various subsidised companies in the 1950s and 1970s shows:

	Actors	Other Staff
LEATHERHEAD (Theatre Club 1952/3)	9	17
(Thorndike 1978/9)	8	40*
SALISBURY (Playhouse 1958)	11	23
(Playhouse 1978)	15	53*
COLCHESTER (Repertory 1952/3)	10	19
(Mercury 1978/9)	10	41*
SHEFFIELD (Playhouse 1951/2)	18	20
(Crucible 1978/9)	27	130

* Excluding bar and catering staff

Some of the proportionate increase in non-performers may be explained by the increasing complexity of theatre production, and much may be explained by the fact that many companies moved into different, sometimes larger premises. Yet it is hard to see why such changes are so *great*, unless the managerial routines of state subsidy somehow induce a greater bureaucracy – which is one of the things opponents of state subsidy within the theatre feared for more than a century. Increasing technical complexity ought to mean fewer employees, not more. And as for the fact that companies have frequently changed premises, it is unfortunately the case that most have moved either from small converted homes, or from old Edwardian theatres, where contemporary notions of efficiency in staffing hardly applied. Again, staffing should have decreased, not grown.

It is hard to escape the conclusion that in the period we have designated "Arts As Welfare", theatre companies expanded their technical, administrative and other support services overmuch. Rather than expand their "output" over time – finding the means of giving more performances to more people each week, for example – they chose to add certain detachable activities such as Workshops, TIE units, Outreach teams, Sunday Night Experimental productions and the like. Such activities have worthy social ends, but contribute nothing to the *central business of the theatre* – showing good drama to the maximum number of people in the best circumstances possible. As economic cir-

15

cumstances have worsened, many repertory companies have had first to drop their "fringe" activities and, then, because actors are easier to drop than other staff, either work with relatively smaller casts on tighter budgets, or shorten the season or – a more frequent solution – so disguise a repertoire season that in fact fewer plays are performed on fewer nights to fewer people than under the old system of fortnightly rep – but the theatre, insofar as its offstage staff are apparently fully employed, still looks misleadingly busy.

An account of the development of the Arts Council of Great Britain gives only a partial view of the nature of theatre subsidy; the impact of local authority support is of equal importance. We have already indicated the importance of local authority funding for amateur theatre, but the effects of local authority involvement in the professional theatre – particularly in the provision of civic theatres – are great.

The *Local Authorities Act 1948* permitted local authorities to spend a discretionary 6d. in the £ of rates on provision for the arts. At first few authorities responded – indeed, in the first financial year following the act, only Sunderland spent the maximum allowed. However, in the 60s and early 70s a number of authorities took advantage of various central government schemes to aid in the rebuilding of civic centres and built theatres. The period of "Arts as Welfare" in Arts Council thinking was matched by the local authorities. In any town of significant size it was common to find the old commercial theatre standing empty, but a new civic theatre opening, which would be built and staffed by the local authority, but would house for at least a part of the year a subsidised repertory company offering the kind of repertoire which would attract an Arts Council grant. At Christmas and at other times it was common for these theatres to "take in" commercial shows. Thus an accommodation was reached between local authorities (providing the venue, and house staff), the Arts Council (supporting the modish notion of artistic theatre work) and commerce (providing at other periods of the year entertainment). Some civic theatres did not, of course, house a repertory

company, but built a programme of commercial runs, "one nighters" of star names, and some subsidised touring shows.

The reasons for the curious division of responsibility are to be found in the practices of local government and the post-war Arts Council. Although local authorities may build and staff theatres, they may not act as promoters – may not, in fact, take any kind of *risk* by mounting theatre productions with ratepayers' money. They thus had to accommodate separately-created charitable companies, which could take production risks and which could receive Arts Council guarantees against loss. For its part, the Arts Council's grant aid included the stipulation that no part of it may be set against the building costs. In many cases this accommodation worked well; in a theatre such as the Belgrade at Coventry, the first post-war civic theatre to be opened, there was a fruitful relationship between Arts Council officers and the local authority, with each playing complementary roles. In other cities there was friction. The Nottingham Playhouse, for example, was at the centre of a complicated row in the mid-60s between the local authority (who both sought a high return in rates from the company housed in their new theatre, and wished for greater control), the Arts Council (who had advised that the theatre be built to a smaller capacity than its directorate wanted, and who were uneasy with the control exercised by its director) and John Neville (who as Director disliked the restraints put on him by his board – comprised of local theatre buffs, councillors and an Arts Council drama officer in attendance – and whose public reaction to that was, quoting his favourite playwright, "O reform it altogether." It ended in the Director's resignation.

In the second kind of civic theatre – those with no resident company – other strains have arisen. The theatre staff, forbidden to produce work directly, feel themselves at the mercy of agents and producers who charge high fees, or take a generous "first call" for performers or shows shoddily produced. They have also found that running a theatre whose staff must conform to local authority payments and practices

INCOME AND EXPENDITURE IN SUBSIDISED THEATRES

REGIONAL DRAMA COMPANY

Local Authority Aid
11%

Arts Council Grant Aid
37%

Box Office Receipts
and other Earned Income.
52%

Production and
Stage Costs
15%

Technical and
Directors' salaries
18%

Administrators'
costs.
31%

Performers'
salaries.
36%

Income

Expenditure

TOURING DRAMA COMPANY

Box Office Receipts
and other Earned Income.
34%

Arts Council Grant
Aid.
66%

Administrators'
costs.
11%

Performers'
salaries.
22%

Technical and
Directors'
salaries.
29%

Production and
Stage Costs.
38%

Income

Expenditure

produces other kinds of financial strains. A theatre works at its peak on Saturdays and in the evenings (unsocial hours), for which local authority staff normally expect to be paid overtime rates. Caretaking, secretarial and technical work can therefore cost the local authority theatre dear, and catering and reception staff, if they are paid under the same agreements as those operating in the local authority's other organisations, can be abnormally expensive, too. There are also great strains in trying to marry theatre practices with those of local authorities in other ways. For example, artistes playing one night stands are paid, directly, on the night of their performances. However, most treasurers' departments will neither write out cheques in advance of the service being given, nor is there any means by which they can issue them after the department closes at 5.30. In this, as in many other respects, managers of the new civic theatres have had to battle to accommodate the two very different worlds of local government and theatre and, in some cases, the asset of receiving a civic subsidy is almost cancelled out by the greatly increased administrative costs the nature of its giving causes.

ISSUES

2.1. Inflated Administrative Costs

IT HAS ALREADY BEEN POINTED OUT IN THE opening chapter that the proportion of expenditure in the theatre paid as actors' salaries has *declined* over the years. That point has been made with running costs, but it can be made just as strongly with commercial production costs, as in this table of a typical West End production budget.

A West End show is financed quite differently from shows presented in subsidised repertory companies, partly because each show is a "one-off", with different cast and director, and partly because it is a separate product which is then "sold" to the management of the theatre in which it is played. In a repertory company the same director and actors will often work on several successive shows, and the finances of running the theatre building and producing the shows the repertory company presents within it are inextricably intertwined. There also exists, of course, the massive difference between the wholly commercial West End, where a play will be run as long as it is profitable, and the state-subsidised repertory company, where any play, however popular, will be seen as a part of a programme over a season, and may well be taken off well before it has exhausted its potential audience.

A West End show's finances are divided clearly into *Production Costs* (the expense involved in rehearsing and mounting the show) and then *Running Costs* (the weekly costs of keeping the show on the stage, including all salaries, repair and cleaning of costumes, set and lighting costs).

Such a play might well cost £20,000 a week to "run" in a major West End theatre, and therefore the takings from the box office need to be well in excess of that figure before a play can move towards its "break even" point, where the "Angels", or "Backers", who have put up the money for the show can have their money back and can begin to see a profit on their investment.

Of course, all box office income in excess of the show's production and weekly running costs is not simple profit. The theatre managers must have their share – usually, in London, this means taking 20% of box office takings, or a weekly fixed sum, perhaps of some £3,000 or so, from the box office. In addition, the theatre's own staff are usually paid by the show's producers. This means that in the West End, to be financially viable a show should usually be playing to audiences of between 60 and 70% of capacity.

In a provincial repertory company's work the attendance figures are sometimes less crucial, in part because the show is budgeted to run for a fixed number of performances and, in part, because many of the production costs are lost within the general (subsidised) running costs of the theatre. Income from the box office is not seen as a repayment of investment and a potential source of profit, but rather one source of income for a budget which should, ideally, balance over a mixed season.

A typical Production Budget for an ordinary play would look like this:

West End Production Budget	
	£
SCENERY	25,000
COSTUMES	10,000
SOUND AND LIGHTING	2,500
SALARIES	15,000
FEES	12,500
THEATRE RENT	12,500
SET AND LIGHTING FIT-UP	8,000
ADVERTISING AND PUBLICITY	25,000
OTHER (REHEARSAL ROOMS, AUDITION EXPENSES, SCRIPTS, MANAGEMENT FEES, ETC.	8,000
	118,500

That difference is particularly crucial when viewed from the perspective of managements of theatres that have a *mixed* programme – sometimes housing seasons of repertory, and sometimes "buying in" touring shows. Those latter may, of course, either be touring versions of recently produced "West End Successes", or specially fitted-up short tours by commercial managements, usually with a TV star or two as the main attraction. In each case the manager of a mixed programme venue has to choose between quite different offers from the would-be users of the theatre. These different arrangements include:

1. The theatre paying a fixed fee to the incoming company, and simply "buying in".
2. The incoming company (perhaps a repertory company playing an annual season), paying a fixed "rental" and taking most, if not all, of the box office.
3. A split of, say, 70% – 30% between production company and theatre management, with the theatre management offering, in addition, a guaranteed figure below which the production company's monies for the week will not fall.
4. Any combination of these.

As will be seen, much time and energy is spent on these variable "deals" which lie behind the presentations in all mixed-programme theatres. The manager faces hard choices, compounded by 1. The growing scarcity of touring productions from which to choose, and 2. The increased volatility of the public – whose likely interest he must shrewdly estimate when making a "deal" – in an economy in which money becomes tighter, and leisure spending more limited.

Throughout the theatre a decreasing proportion of income is spent upon the performers, who might be thought to be the persons most centrally involved with the product. If, for the moment, we lump together the other costs – excepting materials used in the production, the costs of the theatre buildings themselves, and costs of touring – and call them *administrative*, then it will be seen that it is these technical and managerial costs which take up an ever-increasing part of the theatre budget. (This is not to lose sight of the fact that some buildings are shamefully expensive to run and maintain; the annual cost of properly cleaning the Birmingham Repertory Theatre's windows would sustain in grant aid a small touring company.)

There is no doubt that in the narrower sense of the term, theatre administration has become more expensive, simply because the law has made it increasingly complicated. The range of laws and prohibitions which impinge upon a modern administrator is very great. If the administrator runs a building, then it must be built and maintained in accordance with the wishes of the local fire officer, whose authority to inspect the theatre and enforce standards derives from the *Theatres Act 1968*. The administrator must apply for, and obtain, a licence annually from his local authority, who will ensure that the Fire Officer is satisfied before giving permission for the building to open to the public. However, that licence only permits the theatre to present drama, opera and ballet. If the administrator is going to present other kinds of entertainment – variety, for example – the *Public Health Amendment Act 1890* makes it necessary to apply for a music, singing and dancing licence, which is given by a magistrate's court. The administrator must ensure that royalties are paid on all works presented in the theatre, and must fill in a weekly return to the *Performing Rights Society*, giving details of *all* music played in the theatre, on which a royalty must then be paid. Moreover, if commercial sound recordings are used, it is sometimes necessary to obtain an additional licence from the *Phonographic Performance Society (Ltd.)*.

Like all employers, the theatre administrator is required by the *Employers Liability (Compulsory Insurance) Act 1969* to display a certificate showing that he has insured against liability for personal injury or disease. He must also comply with the stringent regulations of the *Health and Safety at Work Act 1974*, which requires, amongst other things, that the theatre should have a safety committee and responsible persons acting as safety officers within each section of the organisation. Unlike many other employers, the theatre administrator has the

WEST END PRODUCTION COSTS
(Prior to opening)

Musical	Play
Scenery and Props 27%	Scenery and Props 22%
Costumes 11%	Costumes 8%
Sound and Lighting 7%	Sound, lights 2%
Fees to Director, Designer, Choreographer 6%	Fee to Director, Designer 11%
Theatre Rent 6%	Theatre rent 11%
Fit up of sets, lights 3%	Fit up of sets, Lights 5%
Travel, Set transport 1%	Travel, set trans. 1%
Printing, Advertising 13%	Printing, advertising and publicity 22%
Management Fees 1%	Management fees 2%
Legal, insurance 1%	Legal, insurance 1%
Rehearsal rooms 1%	Rehearsal rooms 1%
Orchestration 7%	
Salaries for actors, Musicians 16%	Salaries for actors, Musicians 12%

Musical
(Budget, £500,000 upwards)

Play
(Budget, £100,000 upwards)

Booking Information

Theatre Royal, Grey Street, Newcastle upon Tyne, NE1 6BR.

General Manager: J. Michael Grayson.

Telephone (0632) 22061

Box Office open Mon. - Sat. 10.30 a.m. - 7.30 p.m.

Booking opens Monday August 7 for Theatre Royal Club Members.

General Booking opens Monday August 14.
If applying by post please enclose a cheque/postal order made payable to Theatre Royal together with a stamped, self-addressed envelope. Access Barclaycards accepted—simply quote your card number when applying.

Scottish Opera Newcastle Season 78/79. Single ticket booking is also open for the following operas:-

A Midsummer Night's Dream.	6th, 8th December 1978
Seraglio.	7th, 9th December 1978
Katya Kabanova.	23rd, 25th May 1979
Rigoletto.	24th, 26th May 1979

Prices and availability:

	Wed. 13th Sep 6th Dec 23rd May	Thur. 14th Sep 7th Dec 24th May	Fri. 15th Sep 8th Dec 25th May	Sat. 16th Sep 9th Dec 26th May
Stalls		4.00	4.00	
	3.50*	3.50	3.50	
	3.00	3.00	3.00	3.00
Grand Circle		5.00*		
		4.50	4.50	
		3.50*	3.50*	
Upper Circle	3.00	3.00	3.00	3.00*
		2.00*		
Balcony	1.50	1.50	1.50	1.50
	1.00	1.00	1.00	1.00
Boxes (to	18.00	18.00	18.00	18.00
seat 4)	10.00	10.00	10.00	10.00

* single tickets only

N.B. All other seats have been sold by subscription. Guarantee your opera seats and book your subscription before August 7th. Make sure that you take out a subscription next season.

Party Bookings. One free seat for every 10 booked.
Student Standby Tickets. Students may buy any tickets remaining unsold 15 minutes before curtain up at half price.

Travel Subsidy and Arts North Ticket Vouchers
Parties of 10 or more visiting the Theatre Royal from within Northern Arts Association area on any night can claim a subsidy of 50% of the total cost of travel. Minimum fare 20p. Maximum subsidy per party £15. Not applicable to school parties. People under 21 in this area may apply for a book of vouchers under the Arts North Ticket Voucher Scheme which allows them a reduction of 20p from the price of any tickets over 35p.
Further details and application for Travel Subsidy and vouchers from Northern Arts Association, 31, New Bridge Street, Newcastle upon Tyne, NE1 8JY.

Latecomers: In accordance with standard opera practice, latecomers will not be admitted until a convenient pause in the music.

Casts are subject to alteration.

Approximate Finishing Times
Die Fledermaus   10.10 p.m
La Boheme   10 p.m.

The visit by Scottish Opera to Newcastle is part of the national touring programme arranged by, and with financial assistance from Arts Council Touring. Financial assistance is also gratefully acknowledged from the Tyne and Wear County Council and Northern Arts.

SCOTTISH OPERA
Theatre Royal
Newcastle

September 13~16 1978

WEEK 1 of 1978-79 SUBSCRIPTION SERIES

Die Fledermaus

Johann Strauss
In English

Wednesday September 13, Friday September 15 at 7.15 p.m.

Alfred	Dennis O'Neill
Adele	Patricia Hay
Rosalinde	Catherine Wilson
Eisenstein	To be announced
Falke	Malcolm Donnelly
Frank	Gordon Sandison
Orlofsky	Cynthia Buchan
Frosch	John Lawson Graham
Ida	Una Buchanan
Dr. Blind	Peter Bodenham
Conductor	Brian Priestman
Original Production	David Pountney
Restaged by	Graham Vick
Set Designer	David Fielding
Costume Designer	Alex Reid
Lighting	Charles Bristow
Scottish Philharmonic	*Leader* John Tunnell
Scottish Opera Chorus	*Chorus Director* John Currie

Johann Strauss had already achieved fame as a composer of Viennese dance music when he turned to writing operettas, of which Die Fledermaus (The Bat) is the best known. The title refers to the costume worn by Dr. Falke, a friend of Eisenstein, at the last Carnival. Left by Eisenstein to make his own way home in broad daylight in this bizarre costume, the operetta describes his elaborate revenge. As one can expect of 'the Waltz King', the work is full of beautiful melodies, vitality and exuberance, ingredients faithfully reflected in David Pountney's joyful production and translation.

La Boheme

Puccini
In Italian

Thursday September 14, Saturday September 16 at 7.15 p.m.

Rodolfo	Gyula Littay
Marcello	Michael Maurel
Colline	William McCue
Schaunard	Gordon Sandison
Benoit	Norman White
Mimi	Marie Slorach
Musetta	Patricia Hay
Alcindoro	Bruce Budd
Conductor	Robin Stapleton
Producer	Peter Ebert
Designer	Peter Rice
Lighting	Charles Bristow
Scottish Philharmonic	*Leader* John Tunnell
Scottish Opera Chorus	*Chorus Director* John Currie

The loveliest and perhaps the most perfect of Puccini's operas is a moving story of four young people falling in and out of love in nineteenth century Paris. Credible, sometimes funny and ultimately poignant—in this work the composer demonstrates the theatrical brilliance which assures him special respect and affection from operagoers throughout the world.

additional complexity of negotiating contracts for many different kinds of worker – actors, doormen, restaurant staff, cleaners, musicians, technicians, all have different unions and different kinds of agreements – and has, moreover, to deal with what is, compared to other industries, a rapid turnover of staff.

The problems are compounded for those administrators principally concerned with touring for, in addition to finding accommodation, arranging reliable transport and compiling complicated schedules for moving actors and equipment, insurance and contractual matters become much more complicated. In many parts of the theatre business there are complicated agreements to be arrived at between the host theatre and the touring company. Who pays for the various parts of the advertising? Who pays for the telephone calls the company make on their temporary premises? Who pays for the performers' refreshments, or their transport to and from their digs? Costs charged against the touring company, which are subtracted from the agreed payment by the host organisation, are gathered together in what is known as a *Contra Account*.

In their turn, financial matters in the theatre are particularly complicated by *Value Added Tax*, currently paid at a rate of 15% on each ticket sold, which bedevils the myriad minor transactions within a theatre. Small amounts of materials for costumes and sets, re-runs of posters or programmes or mailing leaflets are liable to VAT, which is charged on all the theatre's own services, and paid to nearly all of its suppliers. In this, as in other things, the complexity of the theatre process makes the administrator's task more complicated than that of a manager who employs only two or three kinds of labour, engaged in a limited industrial or commercial process.

These administrative responsibilities, new to a profession some of whose members were as recently as the 1740s still working without proper contracts, keeping the box office takings in a tin and "sharing out" on Saturday nights what was left of them, are, of course, unavoidable. Some of the increasing bureaucratisation of the theatre is less defensible. There is, for instance, the increasing *compartmentalisation* of major productions. This does not come about because of the inherent nature of the drama, but because we have chosen to arrange things like that. If we recall, for example, that each separately constituted company must charge for its own book-keeping, accounting and administration then, by looking at a list of companies involved in one recent small-scale London production, it is not hard to see that such compartmentalisation adds greatly, in hidden administrative costs, to the total expense, and that the cost of intercommunications between interested parties as the show was being rehearsed and produced must also be a considerable additional expense:

- Agency holding the rights of the play.
- The Company holding the lease of the theatre.
- The production company.
- Second production company with whom the first was "in association".
- Two Design teams, both registered as companies.
- Public Relations Consultants.
- Agents of the actors (four agencies, all different).
- Company supplying wigs and hairpieces.
- Company making scenery (painting and assembling).
- Advertising consultants.
- Lighting Designers.
- Sound consultants.

These, of course, are in addition to the many other companies – caterers, cleaning companies and the like – with whom the theatre had longer-term contracts. In a larger-scale production such a list could easily be doubled or trebled. Although the argument for such compartmentalisation must be that of efficient specialisation, it is hard – looking up in a modern theatre at the banks of additional lighting equipment the "Lighting Consultant" thinks necessary to illuminate a box set, or looking at the £300 bill for a simple costume, or the batteries of electronic equipment the "Sound Consultant" thinks necessary to carry the actors' voices to the rear of a theatre far smaller than anything in which Beerbohm Tree, unaided, ever spoke – not to conclude that the specialists justify their status by recommending a sophistication and an expense which is wholly unjustified by the play itself. The lowered costs, increased efficiency, and the more unified artistic results that would seem to follow from bringing all parts of the production process back under one management are compelling reasons for looking for much less compartmentalisation – within the London theatre at least.

Within the subsidised theatre sector, the problems of bureaucratisation are of a different order. There the very business of obtaining grant aid is, as we have noted earlier, often expensive in administrative time; moreover, the recipients of grant aid complain that in return for that support too much time has to be spent filling in forms, "returns", "reports" and financial summaries, all of which wastes time (complainants say much of the information is never used) and, by adding to the administrative costs, further detracts from the purpose for which subsidy is given.

2.2. Overproduction of theatre's raw material

If we speak in the usual terms of efficiency, then the theatre industry has a gross oversupply of its raw material, playscripts, and trains too many actors for the theatre market to offer them reasonable employment. Of the two cases the former seems, on the surface, much less serious. Playwrights have not had an expensive training, and writing plays can be a part-time activity which does not demand membership of a union from anyone seeking to do it for profit. (Although there is, of course, a growing movement to unionise writers and a number of Writers' Unions are listed at the end of this book – but as yet no closed shop.) Circumstances may yet make it an inefficient activity, and one to which we return in a moment when we discuss the bottlenecks in theatre production.

The overproduction of trained actors is a much less tractable difficulty, although it is not a problem inherited from past centuries. Until the early years of this century, and the formation of the Royal Academy of Dramatic Art, actors were not trained as such, but learned the traditional usage of the stage through *ad hoc* apprenticeship schemes. Nor was there, until the formation of the actors' union Equity in 1930, any very effective form of unionisation. Indeed, Equity could not be said to be wholly effective until the 1950s, by which time few, if any, stage performers in receipt of a salary were not fully paid-up members.

The present position is that there are in Britain some 13 Training Colleges for the stage which are members of the Conference of Drama Schools. In addition, some 28 other colleges, 14 polytechnics and 16 Universities offer various kinds of drama course. A number of the students who graduate yearly from such courses dream of performing on the professional stage and, of course, several of the colleges run acting courses which specifically claim to be training students for such a career. However, fewer than a quarter of this student body obtain membership of Equity and with it the coveted "card" that enables them to work professionally.

A newcomer may, if fortunate, be offered work by an existing professional company allowed to give Equity membership each year to one or two people – but, more commonly, the card has to be worked for, either by putting together in bit parts and occasional appearances (a total of 42 weeks' work – the minimum work period which can accompany an application for membership), or by gaining a card through "illegitimate" work in entertainment. This latter entry route arose from the post-war merger between Equity and the Variety Artists' Federation; thus, comedians, strippers and camp entertainers carry the same union card as Shakespearean actors, and a youngster can sometimes exploit skills as an entertainer, gain the card and then work on the "legitimate" stage.

Full membership of Equity by no means carries any guarantee of reasonable employment. At any one time it is likely that four-fifths of Equity members will be out of work, and only a fifth of Equity members earn as much as or more than the average industrial wage from acting. It thus seems to some an almost pointless exercise in bogus professionalism to continue to

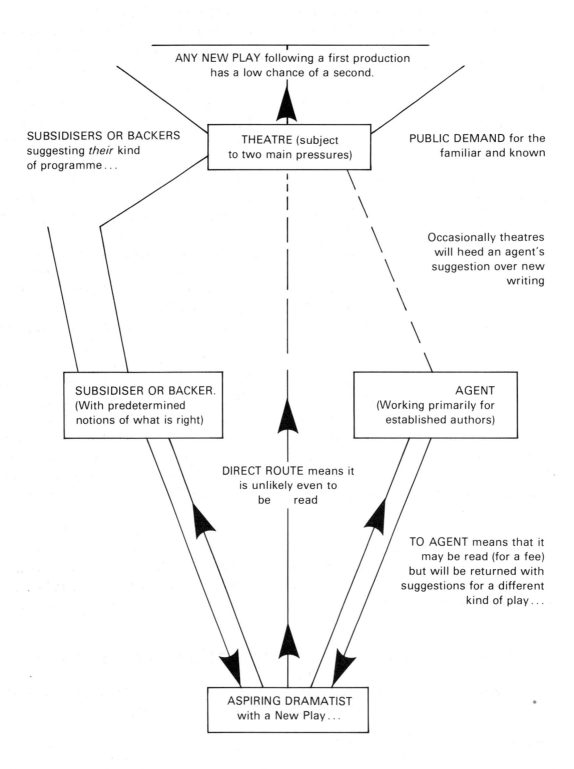

ANY NEW PLAY following a first production has a low chance of a second.

SUBSIDISERS OR BACKERS suggesting *their* kind of programme...

THEATRE (subject to two main pressures)

PUBLIC DEMAND for the familiar and known

Occasionally theatres will heed an agent's suggestion over new writing

SUBSIDISER OR BACKER. (With predetermined notions of what is right)

AGENT (Working primarily for established authors)

DIRECT ROUTE means it is unlikely even to be read

TO AGENT means that it may be read (for a fee) but will be returned with suggestions for a different kind of play...

ASPIRING DRAMATIST with a New Play...

THE "NEW PLAY" BOTTLENECK

restrict entry to the union, and hence to the stage itself. Indeed, a motion to end the closed shop was defeated quite narrowly in 1984 (4,003 votes to 3,498) by Equity's own membership. Their general secretary did point out the likelihood that open membership could produce even less desirable results, and cited the Screen Writers' Guild of America. There, open membership had seen an increase from 27,904 to 54,000 between 1973 and 1983 – but 80% of that membership earned less than $5,000 a year, while 56.5% earned less than $1,000.

2.3. The Production Bottlenecks

The nature of theatre, of course, demands that there should be "overproduction" of play-scripts, because unless there is a range of work to choose from, then any kind of critical process to select the best becomes impossible. Even in a centrally planned and state-regulated theatre economy such as that in the USSR, the theatre department of the Ministry of Culture does not simply instruct an honoured author to deliver a play on such and such a theme by a certain date. Writers everywhere work by inspiration and, to a degree, by chance; the criteria of efficiency cannot be applied to the productive process itself. But the grotesquely unbalanced way in which playscripts of all kinds fail to find their audiences in Britain is, however, wasteful and inefficient. There are three reasons for this: many completed playscripts are not read and considered by the right people, and many are

not read at all; the factors determining the eventual choice of one play for production rather than others are frequently untheatrical, and mean that good plays have decreasing chances of presentation in an industry which, in any case, presents less and less "new" work, and may never have a second. The 1982 European Theatre Subsidy Colliquy noted a European "play mountain" of texts produced under government subsidy schemes and then forgotten. finally, even if a play achieves a first performance, there is now a very good chance it

These constrictions are to a degree interdependant. As they collectively work against the aspiring playwright and reduce his or her chances of successfully breaking into the business, so do they tend to enhance the privileged position of established playwrights.

There are two further bottlenecks within the theatrical process, which affect not only the playwright, but everyone concerned with the theatre industry. The first, which is demonstrated in some detail by the following table, is that throughout Britain the available capacity for presenting professional theatre is steadily declining. Comparisons made broadly over the last 30 years show that in large, medium and small towns the number of theatres, and the number of seats available are in steady, in some cases spectacular, decline. The decline would appear even sharper than this table suggests if we were to show how many theatres which were live for 50 weeks of the year in 1950 are now "dark" for quite long periods during the year.

COMPARISONS IN POPULATION AND PROFESSIONAL THEATRE CAPACITY, 1950 – 1980
(Only theatres which are used by professional companies on a regular basis – more than occasional one night stands – are included)

MAJOR CITIES (EXCLUDING LONDON), 500,000 AND MORE

	1950			1980	
BIRMINGHAM	1,055,000	Alexandra	1775	1,076,760 Alexandra	1367
		Aston		Repertory	901
		Hippodrome	1278	Hippodrome	1952
		Hippodrome	2070	Arts Centre	300
		Repertory	477	Studio	200
		Theatre Royal	2440	(Cannon Hill)	
		TOTAL	**8040**	TOTAL	**4720**

City	Population	Theatre	Seats		Theatre	Seats
GLASGOW	1,128,473	Alhambra	2137	**861,898**	Citizens'	793
		Athenaeum	612		King's	1800
		Empire	1656		Pavilion	1449
		Empress Playhouse	1800		Theatre Royal	1559
		Granada	2206			
		King's	1899			
		King's Park	1300			
		Metropole	1500			
		Park	108			
		Pavilion	1445			
		Princess's	1141			
		Queens	1200			
		Theatre Royal	1985			
		TOTAL	**18989**		TOTAL	**5601**
LIVERPOOL	855,688	David Lewis Theatre	560	**588,600**	Empire	2550
		Empire	3000		Everyman	432
		Pavilion	2000		Playhouse	782
		Playhouse	838		(Studio)	110
		Shakespeare	1380		Royal Court	1525
		TOTAL	**7778**		TOTAL	**5399**
LEEDS	500,000	City Varieties	760	**498,790**	City Varieties	533
		Empire	1540		Grand	1554
		Grand	1500		Playhouse	750
		Theatre Royal	1550			
		TOTAL	**5350**		TOTAL	**2837**
MANCHESTER	700,000	Library	288	**531,270**	Forum	483
		Hippodrome	2000		Library	308
		Opera House	1978		University	300
		Palace	2300		Palace	2000
		Queens Park	1400		Royal Exchange	740
		Chorlton Repertory	300			
		Hulme Hippodrome	942			
		TOTAL	**9208**		TOTAL	**3831**
SHEFFIELD	511,757	Empire	2000	**513,310**	Crucible	1000
		Lyceum	1500			
		Palace Attercliffe	969			
		Playhouse	495			
		TOTAL	**4964**		TOTAL	**1000**

RATIO OF THEATRE SEATS TO POPULATION IN 1950 WAS ROUGHLY 1:87.
IN 1980 IT WAS ROUGHLY 1:174.

MEDIUM-SIZED CITIES
BOURNEMOUTH, HANTS.

	120,000	Hippodrome	1000	**153,000**	Pavilion	1518
		Palace Court	600		Pier	850
		Pavilion	1600		Playhouse	585
		Theatre Royal	1200		Winter Gardens	1818
		TOTAL	**4400**		TOTAL	**4771**
DUNDEE, ANGUS	**175,500**	Kings	1456	**181,000**	Repertory	292
		Palace	1348		Whitehall	750
		Repertory	415			
		TOTAL	**3219**		TOTAL	**1042**
GATESHEAD, DURHAM						
	124,500	Empire	1087	**81,367**	Nil	
		TOTAL	**1087**			
HUDDERSFIELD, YORKS.						
	122,500	Palace	1000	**123,888**	Nil	
		Theatre Royal	1000			
		TOTAL	**2000**			
LUTON, BEDFORDSHIRE						
	103,000	Alma	1639	**162,930**	Library Theatre	256
		Grand	930			
		TOTAL	**2569**		TOTAL	**256**
MIDDLESBOROUGH, YORKS.						
	140,000	Empire	1600	**157,200**	Nil	
		Theatre Royal	1450			
		TOTAL	**3050**			
NORTHAMPTON	**100,000**	New Theatre	1500	**127,460**	Royal	650
		Repertory	833			
		TOTAL	**2333**		TOTAL	**650**
NORWICH, NORFOLK						
	126,000	Hippodrome	1200	**119,600**	Theatre Royal	1275
		Theatre Royal	1850			
		TOTAL	**3050**		TOTAL	**1275**
OLDHAM, LANCS.	**140,309**	Coliseum	670	**104,860**	Coliseum	576
		Empire	1700		Grange Arts	434
		Theatre Royal	1160			
		TOTAL	**3530**		TOTAL	**1010**
PRESTON, LANCS.	**119,600**	Hippodrome	1134	**95,450**	Charter	501
		King's	2028		Lockley	2142
		TOTAL	**3162**		TOTAL	**2643**

ST. HELENS, LANCS.	**100,793**	Theatre Royal	1500	**104,430**	Theatre Royal	707
		TOTAL	**1500**		TOTAL	**707**

STOCKPORT, CHESHIRE

	129,000	Hippodrome	1000	**138,750**	Romily Forum	500
		Theatre Royal	1000			
		TOTAL	**2000**		TOTAL	**500**

WOLVERHAMPTON, STAFFS.

	147,000	Grand	1182	**269,460**	Nil
		Hippodrome	1321		
		TOTAL	**2503**		

RATIO OF THEATRE SEATS TO POPULATION IN 1950 WAS ROUGHLY 1:48
IN 1980 IT WAS ROUGHLY 1:142.

SIX RURAL TOWNS (10,000 – 20,000)
AYLESBURY, BUCKS.

	13,382	County	657	**48,159**	Aston Hall	150
		TOTAL	**657**		TOTAL	**150**

BROADSTAIRS, KENT

	14,000	Bohemia	750	**23,400**	Nil
		Pavilion	600		
		Playhouse	350		
		TOTAL	**1700**		

ILKLEY, YORKS.	**17,500**	Playhouse	150	**24,082**	Nil
		TOTAL	**150**		

LOUTH, LINCS.

	10,000	Playhouse	700	**13,296**	Nil
		TOTAL	**700**		

RETFORD, NOTTS.

	13,420	Majestic	1025	**19,348**	Nil
		Cannon	180		
		TOTAL	**1205**		

TRURO, CORNWALL

	13,000	Regent	639	**16,277**	Nil
		TOTAL	**639**		

NUMBER OF THEATRE SEATS TO POPULATION IN 1950 WAS ROUGHLY 1:16.
IN 1980 IT WAS 1:965.

Some indication of the unused capacity within the subsidised repertory theatres is given in the figures for 1981/2 released by the Arts Council.

ATTENDANCES AND TICKET YIELD IN PROVINCIAL THEATRES (1981/2)
(Main auditorium only)

	No of Perfs	Average Attendance	Percentage	Ticket Yield	Ticket Price
BASINGSTOKE	112	147	38%	2.16	2.51
BIRMINGHAM	263	549	61%	3.07	3.79
BOLTON	256	232	65%	1.76	2.07
BRISTOL	287	472	74%	2.21	2.28
CHELTENHAM	230	388	58%	1.99	2.48
CHESTER	230	266	61%	1.87	2.37
COLCHESTER	245	322	64%	2.75	3.06
COVENTRY	204	363	41%	2.39	3.04
DERBY	240	340	64%	2.19	2.76
EXETER	259	221	51%	2.55	3.27
FARNHAM	378	282	78%	2.70	3.02
GUILDFORD	184	424	75%	3.18	3.75
HARROGATE	218	210	46%	2.23	3.20
IPSWICH	296	294	73%	2.56	3.00
LANCASTER	181	169	67%	2.14	2.56
LEATHERHEAD	294	313	59%	2.82	3.29
LEEDS	182	306	41%	2.61	3.00
LEICESTER	345	445	63%	2.84	3.04
LIVERPOOL EVERYMAN	136	259	66%	1.81	2.13
LIVERPOOL PLAYHOUSE	238	397	52%	2.68	3.05
MANCHESTER CONTACT	200	210	61%	1.73	2.20
MANCHESTER ROYAL EXCHANGE	348	574	82%	3.34	3.63
NEWCASTLE	172	256	57%	2.41	3.22
NORTHAMPTON	287	378	58%	1.91	1.94
NOTTINGHAM	249	420	59%	2.30	2.83
OLDHAM	207	384	68%	2.11	2.45
PLYMOUTH	140	138	31%	2.28	2.44
SALISBURY	290	399	78%	1.97	2.11
SCARBOROUGH	205	199	68%	1.95	2.19
SHEFFIELD	230	592	59%	2.32	2.56
SOUTHEND	213	241	38%	2.45	2.38
STOKE	288	218	56%	1.86	2.54
WORCESTER	189	226	65%	2.38	2.60
WORTHING	339	330	62%	2.18	2.82
YORK	217	426	47%	2.24	2.58

Ticket Yield $= \dfrac{\text{total receipts}}{\text{total seats sold}}$

Ticket Price $= \dfrac{\text{receipts capacity}}{\text{seating capacity}}$

Added to the bottlenecks in programme choice, and the decline in venues and theatre capacity is an associated but different restriction, namely a diminution of *choice*.

In London's West End, where the long run system prevails, the choice is in numerical terms at least as high as ever it was. However, outside London, choice for the consumer is much more severely limited. In part this is because many theatres simply present fewer performances. In the case of the regional theatres, however, it is also because the repertory system in 1950 was largely weekly (the company rehearsing and presenting a different play each week) and this, whatever its disadvantages to actors, gave an impressive repertoire from which to choose. Here, for example, is a list of productions in the Colchester Repertory Theatre in the early fifties:

COLCHESTER REPERTORY THEATRE.
MAIN HOUSE PRODUCTIONS 1952/3

QUIET WEDDING	THE CORN IS GREEN	WHY NOT TONIGHT?
THE DAY'S MISCHIEF	SMILIN' THROUGH	SPRINGTIME FOR HENRY
ARSENIC AND OLD LACE	THE BALLET RAMBERT*	GAYTIME
THE SEVENTH VEIL	THE BIG WINDOW	THE HAPPY PRISONER
HEARTBREAK HOUSE	EASY MONEY	SCHOOL FOR SPINSTERS
MURDER ON THE NILE	THE WHITE SHEEP OF THE	SHORT STORY
NOT PROVEN	FAMILY	THE SAME SKY
THE COCKTAIL PARTY	HOBSON'S CHOICE	THE YOUNG IN HEART
IT WON'T BE A STYLISH	MASTER CROOK	A PRIEST IN THE FAMILY
MARRIAGE	THE THREE SISTERS	WAGGONLOAD OF MONKEYS
RAIN	THE HOLLOW	LADY WINDERMERE'S FAN
THE BIGGEST THIEF IN TOWN	JOHNNY BELINDA	THE WIND AND THE RAIN
MRS. INSPECTOR JONES	WORM'S EYE VIEW	TEN MINUTE ALIBI
COUNT YOUR BLESSINGS	FIGURE OF FUN	THE SEVENTH VEIL†
RING ROUND THE MOON	THE LITTLE FOXES	
WHILE PARENTS SLEEP	WISHING WELL	

* Brought in
† Repeated by demand

The season included some very ordinary stuff, but it also made it possible for people to make their own selection from the repertory, and still go regularly. People who went for a good laugh could choose *Worm's Eye View, Arsenic and Old Lace, While Parents Sleep, Hobson's Choice, The White Sheep of the Family, Why Not Tonight?, Springtime for Henry, Waggonload of Monkeys* and half a dozen more – getting the kind of entertainment they enjoyed in their local theatre at least once a month. Those who enjoyed serious drama could see plays in the same season by T. S. Eliot, Christopher Fry, G. B. Shaw, Chekov, Maugham, Wilde and Williams and could enjoy the fruits of a similar process of choice. It is likely that rep audiences were thus composed of different, interlocking groups, rather than a complete wedge of attenders who went every week, whatever was played.

However, partly to aid the actors – for whom weekly rep was a great strain – and partly in the name of improved production standards, the Arts Council urged its clients first to go fortnightly (or three-weekly) and latterly to adopt a repertoire system – by which three or four plays are held simultaneously in the repertoire and are played alternately for two or three nights each, so that each theatregoer will have a choice of two or even three productions in any one week. It is generally agreed that this has raised the standard of many productions. It is, however, much more expensive to run (the technical changeovers from one production to another are frequent and expensive, and actors who are not in all the productions in the current repertoire are kept kicking their heels on full

pay), and it gives the consumer very much less choice:

COLCHESTER REPERTORY THEATRE MAIN HOUSE PRODUCTIONS UNDER REPERTOIRE SYSTEM 1978/9

PUSS IN BOOTS
BEDROOM FARCE
CHARLEY'S AUNT
SOMETHING'S AFOOT

WORM'S EYE VIEW
COMEDIANS
JUST BETWEEN OURSELVES
THE ROVER

(Plus five *Bought in Tours*. The Colchester Rep. also ran a small studio season in that year, comprising six minority interest productions and four *Bought In Tours*.)

The choice, moreover, is not only to be made from a repertoire 80% smaller than in the early 50s, but its range is narrower. Indeed, it looks rather like the entertainment end of the 1952/3 repertory programme writ large. Ironically, in the name of improving the actor's lot, and of improving standards, we have fewer actors employed, *probably* working at a higher standard, for shorter periods of the year, on a very much *less* interesting programme.

The gradual limiting of consumer choice (and with it, the increasing stress laid by marketing experts upon isolating a single target audience and selling a narrower programme to them) produces a compounded decline in theatre attendances. In all purchases customers prefer to choose from a full range of possibilities. A bookshop which stocks only half-a-dozen authors will not only lose a vast amount of potential trade from people who prefer to read other writers, but it will be unlikely to gain much support even from fans of the authors whom they stock. That is because those readers *choose* to read those writers, exercising a degree of discrimination – a faculty which cannot be exercised if only those authors are offered for consideration. For this reason, as the move to the repertoire system has, by and large, been accompanied by sharply declining attendances, we should consider whether this system has not finally been found wanting, and whether we should not seek to return, at least for some parts of the year, to short-run repertory systems.

2.4. Marketing the Play

The need to provide a reasonable choice for the customers of the industry, which we have been discussing, would seem to be in conflict with a second need. If production costs are to come close to being met, and the downward spiral of more and more subsidy being given to play to fewer and fewer people is to be avoided, then we must seek to exploit the full market potential of each production, and ensure that it is seen by as many paying customers as possible. That would seem to mean long runs. In London the two industrial pressures can be accommodated. The RSC and the National can run full repertoire systems which give their patrons – as their programme is spread over a total of five auditoria – a continuous choice, but in addition can from time to time fully exploit a production by transferring it into the West End (or Broadway) where long runs can be accommodated. The directors of suburban or regional theatres have less room for manoeuvre. They have often only one auditorium and, so, when there is plainly a large public demand, they must either restrict choice by "running" the play, take it off and thus fly in the face of apparent economic sense, or seek to transfer it to a venue where it *can* run. In practice this latter either seems to mean arranging a regional tour at short notice (which is impractical) or (hardly more likely) trying to arrange a West End transfer. On the face of it, this represents one more example of the economic imbalance within the theatre industry between London and the rest of Britain.

The provincial manager is apparently caught by the "wash" effect of theatre sales. During the allotted run of the play interest builds up. If it is successful, then half full houses build to full ones. By the time the growing demand manifests itself, however, the play's planned run in the repertoire is over. Actors are contracted elsewhere. New plays are in rehearsal and different actors contracted to appear in them. (Subscription ticket holders have been, in any case, promised a different show.) Meanwhile, applications come in to the box office, but they cannot be accommodated; they cannot fill the performances that have already, regrettably, played to empty seats. With a tight budget, and with the necessary detailed planning having been transformed into firm contracts, the small theatre company is less free to respond than the management of a large ensemble. The National Theatre, for example, has been able to respond to the great demand to see its production of *Guys and Dolls* by recasting it repeatedly and bringing it back frequently into their much larger and more mobile repertoire, with the result that to date (1984) it has netted £720,000 from its three years on the market.

THE WASH EFFECT OF THEATRE BOOKING IN A LIMITED RUN

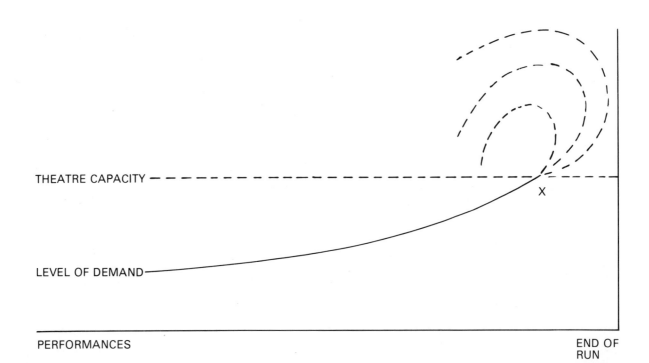

THEATRE CAPACITY

X

LEVEL OF DEMAND

PERFORMANCES

END OF RUN

X is the point at which demand has sufficiently risen to fill the theatre for the later performances. There is, then, a "wave effect" of would-be customers who cannot get in to later performances *falling back* and looking for empty seats earlier in the run.

If the point is reached early in the booking period, then the "wave effect" benefits earlier performances. However, in a short and limited run, for a play whose appeal grows by "word of mouth", its only effect is to leave would-be customers at the end of the run angry because they cannot get in, and the management angry because earlier performances were half empty.

The least exploited way of marketing a successful production to a wider audience is by selling it to television or video companies – or even to an independant company that will not immediately put it on the market but will, under agreement, "store" it for future sales. The latter route has been successfully developed by the RSC, who gain £278,430 from overseas tours, films and "selling" their productions on video – under strict conditions about their eventual marketing. The National Theatre has also found this lucrative, and currently makes £275,000 a year from outside sales, such as those to TV. Plainly the "big two" have the immediate advantage of the "star names", and sufficient breathing space for their actors to accommodate the demands of filming.

Nevertheless there *are* openings for regional theatres to make stronger links with regional TV companies, particularly when seeking to exploit material of particular local interest. It will always be to the TV companies' interests to listen to any approaches from the theatre, in simple economic terms. It currently costs £34,000 an hour to prepare BBC programmes in the normal way, and £50,000 to prepare networked ITV shows. Even allowing for the costs of filming, a regional theatre production which has already aroused local interest will invariably be an attractive proposition. It seems, therefore, in the best interests of both sides to rid themselves of any remaining antagonism between "live" and "media" theatre.

CASE STUDIES

3.1.   The Venue

NO EXAMINATION OF THE THEATRE IN-dustry can ignore the fact that its capital costs are higher than simple logic suggests is right. That is because, just as we continuously close theatre venues, so do we constantly build new venues, often smaller and often in a different style from the older, deserted theatres that they allegedly replace. Whereas few city football grounds have changed location, many cities have seen the disappearance of their old theatres, often from prime sites, and their replacement by different kinds of venue. this is sometimes for commercial reasons – the old Empires and Theatre Royals occupied sites of great potential value to large stores – and sometimes for reasons of ideology. However, the turnover is so rapid that it is estimated that 85% of the theatres in use between 1900 and 1914 in Britain have been demolished or irretrievably altered, and only 9% are still in operation in something like their original state.

In general – and not without irony since the use of the cantilever principle in building theatre balconies would have easily permitted us safely to build them much *bigger* – our theatres have, most markedly since the Ban-crofts' development of a West End style (see p. 38), being built *smaller*. We no longer conceive of a theatre, like Retford's in the eighteenth century, being built so that it could hold virtually the entire population of the town in two performances. We no longer conceive of theatres of the scale of the patent theatres at the time of the 1843 *Theatres Act* holding 3,000 or more. The average size of London's theatres at the turn of the century was a little over 1,000. Now it is just under 700. We have come to believe that small is beautiful, that the pleasures of being a part of a vast concourse are best traded for greater intimacy with the actors.

There is, no doubt, much to be said for such a view – there is a sharper concentration and greater attention to detail, in a small theatre. It has to be said, however, that unless you are able, like the Bancrofts, to charge your smaller audience a very high admission price, it is bound to be uneconomic. It is also frustrating. When a small venue such as the Bush in London produces a hit, it is galling to see potential customers nightly turned away, and to know that it is a condition of *any* success you produce that you must try to sell it to a distant, and probably larger, venue that may be able to exploit it.

We do not, however, change venues simply because we wish to play to a different capacity; we seek change because we wish to perform in a different *way*, to change the relationship be-tween actor and audience. Thus when we look – to take a case at random – at Sheffield, and ask what the advantages were in allowing a good Edwardian theatre, the Lyceum, to close, and to build next to it a smaller modern theatre, the Crucible, it is not enough to conduct the argument solely in economic terms. The back-ers of the new Crucible Theatre (capacity 1,000 as against the Lyceum's former capacity of 1,200) felt that its semi-circular, steeply raked, one-tier auditorium which surrounds its thrust stage, radically changed the nature of the theatre experience, and that this new relation-ship was quantifiably *better* than the relationship in the old theatre, with its traditional box stage and tiered auditorium. If it could be quantified and if, for example, it could be agreed that the new relationship improved the quality of theatre-going by half as much again, then we could begin a simple cost benefit analysis, in which the Crucible would bear the following relationship to the old Lyceum:

(R = former relationship)

| Lyceum | = | $1{,}200 \times R$ |
| Crucible | = | $1{,}000 \times 1.5R$ |

Two further factors which would have to be

introduced early are the building costs (repayment of capital building costs, maintenance, etc.) and some notion of its running costs (costs of manning stage and auditorium fully for a year's programme). There follows the further difficulty of deciding what other factors to include in any such equation (storage space? heating and lighting costs? rehearsal and dressing room accommodation? technical equipment?) and what *weighting* to give the factors: does the nature of space matter so much that its running costs are relatively unimportant, for example.

The question of attempting some cost benefit analysis arises when we turn to our first "case", the building of the new Half Moon theatre in London – a theatre made up of various "streets", thoroughfares in which performances will take place and which are overlooked by "houses", like the medieval theatre. Work started on site for this theatre in May 1983, with over £800,000 in funds from public and private sources already secured.

The complete costs of the New Half Moon are estimated as follows:

	£
SITE PURCHASE	82,000
Interim renovation of temporary theatre during building	42,500
Phase 1. Young People's Theatre	163,000
Phase 2. Main auditorium	652,000
Phase 3. Theatre Equipment	310,000
Phase 4. Conversion to bar and social centre, foyer and box office	30,000
Phase 5. Technical Workshop, extension to auditorium	355,000
Phase 6. Piazza – walkways, etc.	140,000
Phase 7. Social Centre	330,000
Phase 8. Community Gate Towers to Mile End Road	80,000
TOTAL	**2,184,500**

The entire project will be complete by the Winter of 1987.

The enterprise has many management features of note. It is supervised by a carefully constructed appeal committee, 16 strong, which carefully balances impressive names and influential politicians (it is chaired by the deputy leader of the Greater London Council) with hard-working professionals. That is balanced by an in-house design team, all experienced people committed to the Half Moon ideals, comprising the technical director, the general manager, appeal manager, the appeal projects manager and the artistic director. As will be seen from the figures quoted above, the work is divided into eight phases, so the appeal for funds can change gear, with different targets for each stage and, most important, a momentum can be achieved and donors and users can rapidly see the fruits of the development.

By January 1984, £939,500 had been raised, sufficient to build the two auditoria in phases one and two. By that time the appeal had gone out generally, with several ways for interested folk to support the project, according to the amounts they felt able to give (see picture). An attractive leaflet stressed the advantages to donors – tax relief on gross covenanted donations, cost of sponsoring being allowable as a part of a company's advertising budget, credits in publicity, and in-house entertainment for the sponsoring firm's staff among them. On the support already given from public bodies – Arts Council, GLC, ILEA, Borough of Tower Hamlets, Baring Foundation, Chase Charity, City Parochial Foundation – support from the private sector was being built. The roof was on the main auditorium.

The appeals to the public (see appeals leaflet) were imaginative, and in addition to being an effective appeal for money, began to convey something of the sort of place the New Half Moon would be. However, there are still many dangers. Spiralling building costs may set back the project (it takes longer actually to build such a theatre than the much bigger London theatres took to build before the first World War). The enthusiasm may begin to wane. More important than anything else, when should it try to *open* to the public – remembering that first impressions create the "image" to a large extent – and what should its new image be? If the wrong emphasis is chosen, it could go out of mind and die, just as some proud theatres of previous decades have lost their raison d'être and faded away. Is there any competition in its immediate neighbour-

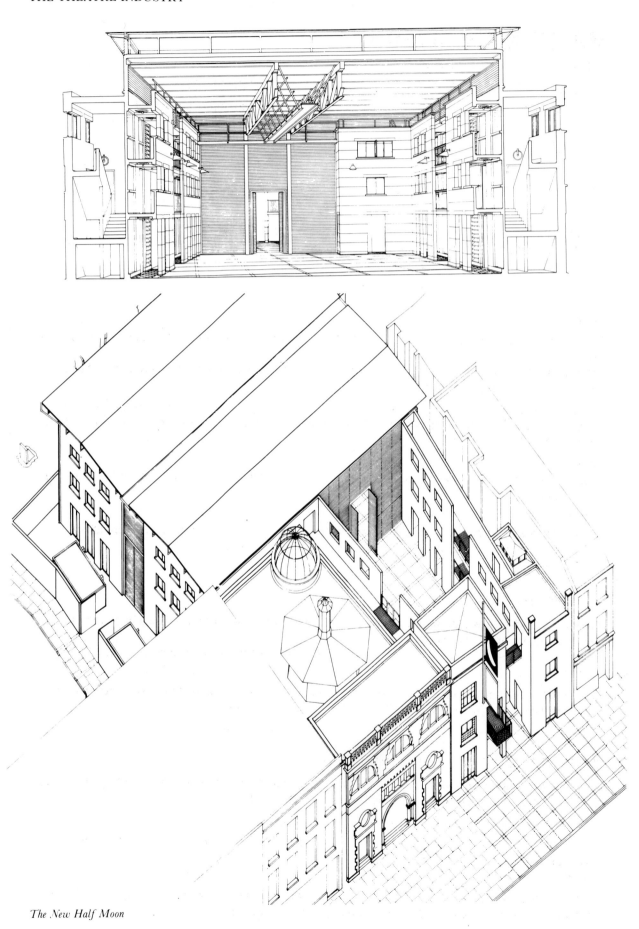

The New Half Moon

MAKE A THEATRE!

THE NEW HALF MOON THEATRE APPEAL

BECOME A LIFE MEMBER OF THE HALF MOON THEATRE CLUB FOR ONLY £10

You will be able to bring 3 guests to any show at the Half Moon for the rest of your life
You will be sent details of Half Moon Programmes on a regular basis for the rest of your life
Priority Booking whenever possible.

Name ....

Address ....

....

I enclose £ .... as the fee for life membership of the Half Moon Theatre Club
NB. If you send us a cheque please make it payable to the Half Moon Theatre New Building Fund
Forms should be returned to the Half Moon Appeal Office, 213, Mile End Rd, London E1

NAME A SEAT!

The Half Moon has long had a name for outstanding performances but desperately uncomfortable seats.
Not only will the new building have comfortable seats, but there will be leg room and perfect sight lines. Isn't this worth supporting?

Please name a seat by donating £250 (or covenanting over 4 yrs) to the Half Moon – Deeds of Covenant are available from the foyer of the Theatre, or from the Appeal Office, 213, Mile End Rd.. London E1. (01-791 1144)

I/We ....
would like to buy a seat and enclose £ ..../Deed of Covenant, to this end for the New Half Moon Theatre.
Address: ....

Please make sure that cheques are made payable to the Half Moon Theatre New Building Fund
and send to the Half Moon Appeal Office, 213, Mile End Rd, London E1.

BUY A BRICK!

Buy a brick of the New Half Moon Theatre! For £25 you can put your name on a brick in the Gate Tower at the entrance of the new theatre.
I .... would like to buy a brick and enclose £ ....
Address ....

NB. Please make sure that cheques are made payable to the New Half Moon Building Fund. Please
return the form to the Appeal Office, 213, Mile End Road, London E1.

RESERVE A PLACE AT THE HALF MOON BAR!

The Half Moon has never had a bar. We will have a restaurant and bar in the new building. Avoid the crush and reserve yourself a place at the new bar now for £50!

A plaque on the bar top will mark your spot!

I .... would like to reserve a place at the new Half Moon bar and enclose £50.
Address ....

Please make sure that cheques are made payable to the New Half Moon Building Fund. Please
return the form to the Appeal Office, 213, Mile End Rd , London E1.

39

hood that could suddenly emerge and render it obsolete?

3.2. Theatre Prices

As in many other areas, the welfare notion that theatre should be widely available is in conflict with the straightforward economic arguments when levels of ticket pricing in the theatre are considered. There is, on the one hand, a feeling that theatre ticket prices should not be so high so that no-one is reasonably deterred by them, that they deter the less privileged in particular. On the other, there is the knowledge that theatre admission prices have fallen behind in the rate of increases of other non-essential purchases in recent decades, and that the industry is failing to maximise its potential box office income.

COMPARISON OF PRICES, 1910 and 1980

200 CIGARETTES COST	*30 times*	as much in 1980
BOTTLE OF SCOTCH COSTS	*24 times*	as much in 1980
THEATRE STALL COSTS	*6 times*	as much in 1980

That is particularly true of the top prices. An equally significant trend over the same period has been the gradual erosion of the difference between top and bottom prices. The average lowest price in theatre in 1910 was around 1s. 2d. – nearly 6p. – and it is now (on a broad average over the country) just under £3.00. *The cheapest seats have therefore multiplied over the same period by some 116 times!* If a pint of beer had increased at *that* rate, it would now cost the same as the cheapest ticket to a good theatre, rather than its present, much lower, cost.

Such figures, of course, are derived from large established building-based theatres with conventional pricing structures. There are many exceptions to this broad historical comment. Some groups work either for audiences which pay nothing, or work within touring grids that enable them to be seen at admission charges of 75p, £1.00 or £1.50. Many groups structure their pricing system so that the elderly, young people, the unwaged and other disadvantaged groups are admitted at low cost.

There is little absolutely reliable information on the impact of price variation which leads to a single impelling conclusion. That is because there are other factors in the equation, and the theatre performances that are being compared are invariably of different natures, which may have had greater effect than changes in pricing. There are cases showing that theatre attendances rise when a community has *less* marginal spending power, even though ticket prices have remained constant – but that merely shows that the local theatre-goers have prioritised theater-going in the more limited leisure activities they choose between. Equally, there are many cases where increased prices dramatically raise attendances, and numerous cases, too, of people refusing to go to a show even when it was offered free – cases of the ticket price being strongly associated with the *value* of the product. In this respect our second "case", that of the pricing policies pursued by the Citizens' Theatre, Glasgow, is of particular interest.

The low seat price scheme at the Citizens' is a central aspect of the policy of the theatre and company. In 1970 the present Citizens' Company was formed by Giles Havergal and Philip Prowse (later joined by Robert David MacDonald) under the chairmanship of William L. Taylor, to present "conceptual" interpretations of classical and twentieth century texts with a young company of actors all paid the same. This policy continues and as well as its own company productions, the Citizens' produces a Christmas Show and presents a short season of visiting companies.

The theatre is a traditional three-layer Victorian one with 800 seats. In 1974/75 seat prices were on a conventional "tiered" system from £1.20 down to 50p. (VAT and RPI adjusted to January 1984, these would be £4.38 down to £1.82.)

In September 1975, the 50p for all seats policy was introduced. School children and students paid 25p. The idea of the cheap seat price came originally from a notion that theatre should be free, but this proved unrealistic politically. However, the crucial factor was the belief that as a subsidised amenity the theatre was already being paid for twice by people living in Glasgow and Strathclyde Region through taxes and rates and, therefore, those using it should pay as little as possible the third time round.

The seat price stayed at 50p for three seasons, then rose 75p (with 50p concessions) for two seasons before edging its way up to 90p (60p concessions) for 1980/81 and 1981/82. For the past two seasons it has been £1.50 with concessions at £1 and the 1984/85 season price is £2. Concessions are still £1 and OAPs and unemployed can get in free on the door. All shows have a free preview.

The annual Christmas Show has always had a conventional higher seat price structure (in 1984/85 from 50p to £3). Although the "commercial" aspect of the Christmas Show is more dominant than with the season, the general idea of trying to keep seat prices as low as possible in order to increase accessibility is retained.

In the first instance, no significant administrative changes were made in operating the new pricing policy – the ticketing and booking system remained the same on a conventional three-part "Harlands of Hull"-type ticket. This has since changed, although not as a result of the pricing policy.

From the time the policy was introduced, attendances have increased. For example, total audience figures (including the Christmas Show) over the period 1971 to 1975 compared with 1980 to 1984, show average attendance per performance has risen from 391 to 529. The increase has not been unswerving, but the general trend is clear.

The scheme has also seen a broader age and social range in the audience. The last fully scientific survey was carried out in 1977, so recent evidence depends on empirical observation, but there seems little doubt that the cheapness of the policy has had an impact on not only how many people come, but who they are. Moreover, the pricing policy has had some effect on the attitude of the audience. This is relevant to the repertoire presented by the Citizens', in that people seem more prepared to take a chance with an unknown play or an unconventional production if the price is low. This has allowed greater flexibility in programming.

It may also be true that the pricing policy combines with other elements at the Citizens' (in the rougher part of town there is something unconventional in a theatre which is red and plush with mirrors on the inside, but looks like a bomb site from the outside) to create an atmosphere whereby the attitude of the audience is different from elsewhere.

The basis of the seat price policy has always been that it must work in financial terms. From 1973/84 to 1983/84, earned income increased by 324%, grants by 239% and the retail price index by 238%. Earned income is not only seasonal box office, but greater trading profit generated by higher attendances, as well as interest earned at the bank and Christmas Show receipts. The policy has had its critics – including the Scottish Arts Council, the main funder of the theatre – who have met the response that as long as more people are coming in, artistic standards are maintained and income is going up by more than grants and inflation, and the books are balanced, then individual aspects of the policy are for the Board and executive to decide.

The scheme has had its disadvantages, of course. Firstly, it does not *guarantee* high attendances or greater accessibility. A play with good notices, even with the accumulated reputation and goodwill of the Citizens' Company after 15 years and with low seat prices, can still have the occasional performance when attendance does not reach the 150 mark.

There is also the possibility that the low seat price has put some people off and that a more regular audience and steadier income could have been built up if, for example, there was a higher price with greatly reduced concessions. In other words, the concept could be that instead of theatre as a subsidised amenity costing as little as possible for everyone when they avail themselves of it, it should instead charge a higher price to those who can pay while remaining equally accessible to those who cannot.

Another disadvantage arises from the way in which the scheme was applied as a one-price scheme, particularly in a Victorian theatre with restricted view seating. On such a basis, the price charged has to be judged reasonable for the worst seat behind a pillar, or at the back of the gallery. However, low ticket prices and all-over-the-house-same-price schemes are not the same thing and it would be perfectly possible to have the former without the latter. There is no question that the low seat price is much more important than the all-over-the-house aspect, in that it reflects the vital philosophy of the Citizens' as a subsidised theatre.

It is important not to interpret the experience at the Citizens' literally into every other situation – the "we would love to charge as little as you do but we would never get away with it" syndrome. As well as the other points mentioned, the other indispensable aspect of the whole scheme is seeing the box office as a creative part of the operation, no less than the designs for the set, the choice of actors or plays. It is rooted in the Citizens' artistic policy, but it is also related to the theatre's geographical position. Were the management running the Citizens' now elsewhere, they might adopt a very different policy towards seat pricing, but the essential of taking it as a creative decision and part of the overall policy of a subsidised theatre would remain.

One of the key elements that does seem to be generally applicable is the scheme's simplicity, both for the public and the staff. People know exactly where they stand (and it is a lot easier to fill in house returns).

Reserved advance/unreserved doors system

Against a background of reduced funds in the arts generally, the Citizens' Theatre wanted to put as much money on product and as little on administration as possible, in order to prevent "the tail wagging the dog".

In September 1982, a number of administrative changes were effected, including the closing of the tea-room and bookstall, the streamlining of the trading operations in the theatre, the reduction of rehearsal time, the simplification of the mailing process (no more envelopes, just postcards for press and schools information) and changes in the box office and booking system. Some of the experiments worked, others didn't, and by 1984/85 the less successful ones had been dropped.

For the 1981/82 season of Citizens' Company productions, the audience coming on the door was as high as 70% of the total attendance. This caused problems in trying to run a conventional printed ticket reservation system on the doors without holding up the start of the show. In other words, the audience seemed for the most part to treat the theatre as they did the cinema. The Citizens' decided to try and follow suit with the box office system.

For parties booking in advance, an invoice is made out with most of the pro-forma details preprinted on a no-carbon-required, four-copy sheet. Dates and play title are written in by hand. Advance booking for individuals is on a three-part, no-carbon-required voucher, again printed with most details but with dates and title written in by hand. Plans are used and reservations marked on them. The corresponding seats are "stickered" each evening (with a Velcro-attached plastic envelope containing a card marked "Advance Booking") immediately prior to the advance box office closing and the doors box office opening at 6.00 p.m. From 6 p.m., automatickets are sold from the small front box office at the entrance to the theatre in the outer foyer. These do not specify any seat or area in the theatre, but simply give a price (either full price, or £1 for concessions, or complimentary for OAPs and unemployed). Anyone with a reserved seat ticket booked in advance goes to that seat; anyone with an automaticket is advised that they can sit anywhere there is not a sticker.

After many hiccups the system has now been refined and administratively the advance booking does not seem to take any more time than it used to. The doors booking is much quicker and the queues can be dispersed in a matter of minutes. The check at the door of the theatre has to be more careful than in the past and the front-of-house staff have to be more alert than they might otherwise have to be if all the ticketing system was reserved.

However, the doors automaticket system has worked well and does co-exist fairly smoothly with the reserved system. Even on a busy Saturday night, contests over whose seat belongs to whom have been extremely rare and people have generally respected a coat over a seat, or even a one-sheet programme perched on its edge, as a mark of reservation. (Nor do bar takings seem to be down as a result of people clinging on to their seats and not going for a drink.)

It has proved necessary to have the facility of a back-up voucher system on the doors, but this is used only for telephone bookings and for friends, guests of the theatre who wish to have seats held. A deadline of 6.45 p.m. is given. The voucher for this is preprinted, but is only a two-sheet, no-carbon-required voucher. The vast majority of door sales are still unreserved automatickets.

Free seats for the unemployed

In January 1982, after careful consideration by the Board and with the funding bodies, the Citizens' introduced a pilot scheme of free seats for the unemployed. The scheme was agreed on the condition that it was only available on the doors and it was not used for the Christmas Show. People presenting themselves as unemployed must show a current UB40 card.

The scheme was also approved on the basis that it did not adversly affect box office income and that it was monitored carefully.

Unemployed tickets now form 8% of the audience. A record of how many people in each category attend, including unemployed, is kept for each performance and a vox-pop mini survey was carried out shortly after the scheme was introduced, in particular to find out whether the scheme was attracting genuine newcomers (about half of those questioned said they would not have come if they had had to pay).

The scheme seems to have attracted considerable goodwill (and also some criticism) and when first introduced received a lot of media and press coverage, both locally and nationally.

Any individual booking in advance pays full price.

£1 tickets booked in advance represent mostly school and student parties.

Ticket Centre is the four outlets around central Glasgow run by Glasgow District Council Halls Department. Only full price tickets can be bought from a Ticket Centre.

OAPs and unemployed concessions are available on the doors only.

This covers all plays (eight Citizens' Company and four visiting company productions) from 1 April 1983 to 31 March 1984, but excludes the Christmas Show which has a different price structure and mostly advance bookings.

The total attendance for the season (i.e., represented by 100% above) was 76,595.

A more detailed breakdown shows that the better attended a production, the higher the proportion of advance booking.

Similarly, the better attended a performance (e.g., Saturdays compared to Mondays) the higher the percentage of advance sales.

All bookings made in advance are reserved seats, for which a voucher (or invoice in the case

CITIZENS' THEATRE LIMITED, GLASGOW
Box Office Breakdown 1983/84

	Advance	Ticket Centre	Doors	Totals
£1.50	28%	8%	29%	65%
£1.00		10%	19%	
COMPS: GUESTS, STAFF AND PRESS	4%	–	1%	5%
COMPS: OAPs	–	–	3%	3%
COMPS: UNEMPLOYED	–	–	8%	8%
TOTALS	**41%**	**8%**	**51%**	**100%**

CITIZENS' THEATRE LIMITED, GLASGOW

Season	Seat Price (Season)	Seat Price (Xmas)	No. of p'fs	Total atten- dances	Total earned income £	Total revenue subsidy £	Surplus/ (deficit) for year £
1971/72			235	78,843	35,629	82,570	(240)
1972/73			201	87,918	41,195	97,469	7,731
1973/74	40p to £1.10	40p to 90p	189	82,407	47,613	119,642	9,777
1974/75	50p to £1.20	50p to £1.10	232	86,319	51,174	142,500	(1,725)
1975/76	50p (25p)	60p to £1.20	222	108,658	69,682	183,000	11,690
1976/77	50p (25p)	70p to £1.40	227	120,840	79,580	216,000	(493)
1977/78	50p (25p)	80p to £1.55	235	123,203	84,971	235,000	(798)
1978/79	75p (50p)	90p to £1.75	183	94,995	86,728	275,000	(3,011)
1979/80	75p (50p)	75p to £2	203	125,263	124,457	304,000	3,687
1980/81	90p (60p)	90p to £2	203	112,231	138,649	324,500	4,889
1981/82	90p (60p)	£1 to £2.80	208	111,874	147,679	352,475	3,235
1982/83	£1.50 (£1)	£1 to £1.50	223	103,879	127,846	382,973	–
1983/84	£1.50 (£1)	50p to £2.50	228	127,704	201,791	406,180	1,801

of groups) is given. The corresponding seats in the auditorium are "stickered" for each performance covering all the advance bookings. The remainder are free for door sales, which are non-reserved and sold as in a cinema with an automaticket.

What lessons are to be learned from the pricing policies of this extraordinary theatre?

3.3.　Theatre Attendances

Although the proportion of the population visiting the theatre has been in steady decline for at least three decades, and although the proportion of leisure spending on theatre-going continues to sink, the history of the theatre industry suggests that such trends can be reversed. The theatre, after all, reorganised itself totally in the seventeenth century, after being banned for 18 years; it survived the coming of the mass cinema chains, the depression and – in fine order – two devastating world wars. It is, therefore, by no means impossible that it will not only survive television and current economic slumps, but that it may re-form itself and become again what it was in the time of the first Elizabeth and again in the mid-nineteenth century – the most popular of the serious arts.

It is easy to forget in a welter of gloomy headlines that theatre-going is still, over a year,

more popular than going to watch soccer or cricket. However, one must not overstate what is still a minority activity; on any evening of the year there are still more people in Her Majesty's prisons than there are in Britain's professional theatres. In broad terms the figures are these:

ANNUAL ATTENDANCES AT BRITAIN'S THEATRES IN THE EARLY EIGHTIES

AMATEUR THEATRES	15,000,000
SCHOOL, COLLEGE, UNIVERSITY PERFORMANCES	3,500,000
TOTAL AMATEUR ATTENDANCE	**18,500,000**
WEST END THEATRE ATTENDANCE	**8,800,000**
SUBSIDISED REPERTORY THEATRES (Main auditorium)	3,400,000
(Studios)	120,000
SUBSIDISED TOURING COMPANIES	200,000
SUBSIDISED TIE/YPT COMPANIES	150,000
TOTAL SUBSIDISED THEATRE ATTENDANCE	**3,870,000**

(All these figures should be treated with caution. Those for amateur theare are derived from the nationwide survey undertaken by CCAT in 1979/80, and raised by 5% to suggest the likeliest 1981/82 figure. The figure for the West End – which the Society of Theatres now claims has risen – was from a survey commissioned by SWET at that time. The figures for subsidised theatres 1981/82 were released by the Arts Council of Great Britain. All have been rounded up.)

Such figures do not, of course, tell us very much about our theatre audiences. It is meaningless to say that on average one in three persons goes to the amateur theatre each year, because such a general figure does not show the size of the "core" audience that goes regularly, nor that of "occasional" audience which goes two or three times a year (it seems likely that the amateur theatre was a dedicated core of attenders loyal as any professional patrons; the CCAT survey estimated that the amateur theatre had nearly 200,000 patrons and associates, more than the total which sits on professional theatre boards.) However, we do not know enough about professional audiences to give more than meaningless statistical generalisations. Those audience surveys available – albeit carried out largely in London – suggest that a slight majority of the population now never go to the theatre at all, and that at the other end of the scale there is a minority, probably now little more than one in a hundred of the urban population, that goes *very* regularly – once a fortnight, or more frequently.

Of course, just as it will not do to talk of "the audience" in over-generalised terms, nor will it do to talk of "the theatre" as if it is all one entity. It is certainly not enough to chop it up into "West End", "Subsidised" and "Amateur", not only because there are other categories, but because within each of these are subdivisions which sometimes straddle amateur and professional, or West End and subsidised forms. Take, for example, the public's liking for musicals. It is frequently the case that medium and large provincial theatres find that the largely amateur production by the local operatic society provides one of the best draws of the year – and that same popularity is keeping the West End afloat – more than a dozen musicals are running at the time of writing – and proving a considerable aid to the National Theatre's fortunes, with their highly successful *Guys and Dolls*.

There are, around almost every theatre, an interlocking series of potential audiences, different groups of people who will react positively to pantomime but won't watch modern dramas, to pop concerts but not music hall, to musicals but not light comedies, and to Shakespeare but not Shaw. If the theatre is to know its audience, it must manifest itself in many different forms. It will not do, as some disillusioned arts bureaucrats have done, to announce that "the" audience for "the" theatre is of such-and-such a predetermined character. People must have choices, and they must be given time to adapt leisure habits. Moreover, we must constantly remember how dramatically theatre-going habits can alter. When sitting in a near-empty auditorium at the Sheffield Crucible (currently going through a bad patch) it is sometimes heartening to remember that only 30 years before, Harry Hanson's weekly rep in the Lyceum next door ran its "Popular Plays at Popular Prices" to virtual capacity, week after week, *twice nightly!*

In essence, our theatre marketing has to choose between two quite different purposes. Should it aim, over time, to draw back the *potential* audiences – those people who are by no means hostile to a good night out in a theatre, but who nowadays probably only go to such live performances when on holiday (surveys suggest a much larger proportion of people go to all kinds of theatre experiences when they are away from home), or should it be to draw in, as efficiently and as profitably as possible, the committed theatre-goers? The first approach suggests: varied, frequently-changing programme; widespread scatter of advertising materials, and varied approaches; maximum number of selling points; varied ticket pricing structures; and a tendency to sell the location alongside the events.

Whereas the second approach suggests: carefully-chosen, limited programme; highly targeted advertising, written and presented for special groups; strategic selling points of high efficiency, placed to benefit target groups; single price bands, or subscription sales in "packages";

and a tendency to sell the socialising which accompanies the events.

Few theatre organisations fall neatly into one or other of these categories. Although a theatre may be running a subscription scheme it usually has half an eye on its general audience potential, and few theatres with a broad, populist approach shun building up specialist mailing schemes.

In our two short "cases" the first, a marketing scheme adopted by SWET, may be said to have many elements of the first category, whereas the second, a subscription scheme, has many elements of the second. The contrasts between them are interesting.

The Leicester Square Half Price Ticket Booth

The aim of this booth, based on a similar one in Times Square in New York, is to sell seats on the day of performance which are part of the unused capacity of West End theatre. Interest in the shows is generated by the general advertising campaigns of SWET, which involve extensive newspaper advertising, poster advertising (including special campaigns selling the general notion of London theatre-going, as well as panels listing details of all West End shows), television advertising, radio, leafleting and other publicity. The booth itself is promoted in some campaigns as a special selling point, but heavily relies on passing trade for its custom.

Participating theatres give a number of unsold tickets to the booth on the day of performance. The names of shows for which tickets are available are then chalked on a board, which is not readily visible from the rear of a long queue (in New York it is arranged so that it is actually impossible to see the named shows until one has worked one's way near to the head of the queue). Those shows for which tickets are available – between five and 10, usually – are taken from a West End programme of 30 to 40 plays and the prospective purchaser's choice is thus limited. However, tickets are sold at half price, which compensates for the limited range.

In 1983, the last year for which full figures

are available, the booth sold an estimated 12% of the overseas tourist trade in tickets – suggesting that visitors who do not know London's geography well may particularly welcome it – and an estimated 3% of the UK trade. On average, each purchaser took two tickets or more, and the average price paid was £5.46. (Some of the most popular London shows, which do not need to sell tickets at half price, calculate their average sale is four or five tickets per purchaser, which suggests that families and *groups* of friends are willing to pay more to visit the single show they have collectively chosen.)

Some theatre managers have feared that by selling off unused capacity cheaply that they may be losing a "passing trade" which would have bought the tickets full-price at the theatre itself. However, a significant number of people have told researchers that if they had not bought tickets in this way they would not otherwise have gone to the theatre, and in 1983 it was estimated that the ticket booth generated additional sales of 135,000 tickets, and a *net* increase to West End theatre as a whole of some £95,160.

Subscription Series in Newcastle upon Tyne

Scottish Opera wished, in particular, to promote their 1979 season at Newcastle, which would consist of three one-week visits during the year; partly to promote Newcastle as their "second home", and partly to counter the threat from the then newly-formed ENO (North), based in Leeds, which was looking to extend its own natural catchment area. The theatre seated 1,281, and the company was to perform four times in each of its three visits during the year.

A careful price structure was agreed in 1978, and the subscription scheme launched during a "sell-out" week of the company's work in April of that year. The campaign was thus from the start heavily targeted on the existing opera-lovers who were already a committed audience. They were reached by mailing lists, and by supplementary advertising by poster, newspapers, leaflet drops, etc. For an initial three months tickets could *only* be purchased by entering the subscription scheme. The advertising leaflet is set out on pages 46 to 49.

In July 1978, at the end of the three months of closed subscription booking, the box office figures were as follows:

TOTAL NUMBER OF SEATS AVAILABLE FOR EACH WEEK	5,124	
TOTAL NUMBER SOLD BY SUBSCRIPTION	2,766	54.0%
TOTAL NUMBER OF SEATS REMAINING	**2,358**	
LESS HOUSE AND PRESS SEATS	248	4.8%
LESS REMAINING GALLERY SEATS	790	15.4%
TOTAL NUMBER OF "GOOD" SEATS LEFT EACH WEEK	**1,320**	**25.8%**

And each of the weeks broke down as follows:

	Weds.	Thurs.	Fri.	Sat.
SOLD BY SUBS.	824 (64%)	476 (37%)	559 (44%)	907 (71%)
HOUSE & PRESS	74 (6%)	74 (6%)	50 (4%)	50 (4%)
SEATS REMAINING	383 (30%)	731 (57%)	672 (52%)	324 (25%)

The advantages to the theatre were that 54% of its seats were safely sold by the time the more chancy public booking opened and, that, by early selling of 11,064 seats, the theatre now had £39,456 in the bank. Moreover, it had built up a very good list of its highly-committed "core" audience.

As with the half price ticket scheme, however, one must query whether a different method of selling might not be more profitable, in all senses. Is the additional cost to the box office staff less than the cost of simply borrowing money and paying interest? And, as the previous year had seen sell-out programmes, would the houses not eventually have comfortably filled and yielded, over the longer term, higher income? Conversely, the proponents of such schemes could argue that there is in the purchase of subscription schemes a significant number of people who would not otherwise have bought tickets at all. Finally, and most important of all, are such targeted schemes working to the ultimate detriment of theatre by targeting upon an ever-smaller, more closely defined group of theatregoers who may one day either change their habits or have insufficient resources to pay the increasingly large sums membership of such schemes demand?

It might be said that the theatre's prime aim in all management should be once again to say that the theatre public is no different from *the* public, and that a minority pursuit has once again become a majority pleasure.

DEVELOPMENT OF THE INDUSTRY

IT IS MORE THAN USUALLY DIFFICULT TO forecast the future of the theatre industry. It does not produce goods, nor is it a service. People do not need drama in the same way that they need food and, providing theatre is not a part of the welfare services in the way that education or the health service are. In essence, theatre-going is a curious, ancient, ultimately irrational activity. The relationship of audiences to the drama cannot be discussed in quite the same way that purchasers can be quantitatively related to the food and drink that they buy and consume; nor can it be analysed in the way that doctors and their patients are. Audiences are bound to the drama by a curious kind of *aesthetic contract*; neither side is wholly dominant, *neither* side is the simple purchaser and the other the goods or service. By its nature, theatre may suddenly grow, may pulse with renewed life, just when every economic indicator suggests that it should be left for dead.

In suggesting several broad areas of development, therefore, the writer can only point to trends which seem undesirable, and suggest that the theatre *may* flourish if they are reversed. You can suggest, likewise, various positive developments which *may* give a basis for growth. But you cannot make it happen, nor can you guarantee that prohibition and bad managerial practice will necessarily preclude, against all the indicators, a genius who will transform our theatre once more. Shakespeare's theatre was banned from the City of London, and had to be built at an inconvenient spot, which meant that for many of his audience the cost was doubled by having to pay to be ferried over the river. He had to run a repertoire system that imposed demands upon his writing, and the actors' rehearsal time, which a contemporary company would find totally impossible. He had no advance booking system, and could do little financial forward planning. His houses were –

except for holidays – variable, and the whole enterprise was dependant upon decent weather. Yet that theatre not only flourished, but shines down the years as a supreme theatrical achievement. What management expert, at its birth, would have forecast anything but ruin for the whole enterprise?

Bearing this warning in mind, however, it must still be said that the British theatre seems to be destroying itself, not because of the fact that its performers make it labour-intensive, but because it has chosen to organise itself so that the non-performers cost too much. It is not uncommon to sit in a tiny audience reading a grotesquely over-elaborate theatre programme in which you will discover that more people are actually engaged in marketing and promotion than appear on stage.

A significant factor in this is the absurd technical dressing-up of what is a simple human art. The great theatres of Ancient Greece had no lighting nor sound equipment, but were central to their civilisation. Our theatres, which have become peripheral to ours, contain too much lighting and sound equipment for the simple purposes that the drama ultimately requires of them. And, as we have said earlier, such technical dressing-up of theatre has brought with it vastly increased wage bills for the necessary experts to operate the unnecessary technology. More insidiously, the technology in our theatres may actually detract from the excitement – certainly the breakdown rate of the equipment installed in our major theatres introduces an unwelcome chanciness in our theatre-going experience. (The National Company has suffered many tribulations through its vastly expensive technical machinery failing to produce effects which would have been routine in a provincial Victorian theatre; its stage, for instance, does not, in spite of all our technical expertise, actually revolve.) And it gets in the way of the human business of theatre. When actors in the RSC's Barbican theatre forget their lines, the prompting is done by a distant ASM *over the loudspeakers*. The design of the stage, with its bristling technical appendages, allows of no other than this dreadful embarrassing solution to something a Victorian company managed simply and discreetly. In our theatre-building, in our equipping of theatres, in their redesigning, we need to look to a simpler, less expensive form of stage management.

Too many of our theatres have been built too small. A mixture of feelings – most prominent among them being the assumption that large-scale theatre is invariably cruder, and therefore worse, than small-scale work – have led our civic planners and theatre architects to assume that theatres must be smaller than in the last century. This is bound up with a fatalistic feeling that the box office can never again pay for theatre costs (except in the West End, of course). Neither feeling is necessarily justified. Sophocles is a greater dramatist than Arnold Wesker, though he wrote for audiences of 20,000 and Mr. Wesker must write for a few hundred. And there has sometimes been the sense that the experts' advice to keep theatres relatively small has been bound up with their wish to keep them under experts' control, and not to have them responsive to the popular taste. Had John Neville had his way, for example, the Nottingham Playhouse would have had 200 more seats in it than Arts Council experts advised. It is, then, arguable that it would not in the first years have needed Arts Council grant aid at all, but could have sustained itself commercially. For a larger auditorium, production costs and the running expenses of the play remain the same; costs of manning the house rise only marginally. Therefore the profit on those extra 200 seats would have been very much greater. Whenever we have the chance to build or rebuild our theatres we need to look again at the conventional wisdom of the last 30 years and remind ourselves of the *advantages* of having great public theatres rather than small, intimate ones.

The theatre is plainly in need, not of more marketing, but of better-directed marketing efforts. Plainly, the growth of so-called expert marketing in the theatre in recent years has been something of a disaster; appointments of specialist marketers have risen in almost a direct inverse ratio to the decline in audience numbers. This is partly because we have too readily surrendered to the view that popular taste is always inferior to the judgement of experts, and theatres have found themselves making up programmes which please the experts (hence ensure their grant aid) but displease large numbers of their potential audience. Subsidisers are always pushing towards the avant garde, the minority interest drama – and, by yielding to their pressures, theatres have given their marketing experts some unsaleable programmes to "market". But the marketers themselves have often gone down the wrong path. They have concentrated upon the methods of targeting the known theatre-going audience, and selling hard to them, rather than upon *spreading* their catchment. Mailing lists for known customers only, targeted leaflet distribution, carefully targeted subscription schemes which threaten to exclude the casual attender – all such methods run the risk of concentrating upon making a shrinking audience pay more and more, rather than an expanding audience paying less.

Where theatres are successful – Barry Stead's Nottingham Theatre Royal, Dick Condon's Norwich Theatre – they are nearly always large, with varied programmes that are not ashamed to exploit the vulgar and popular as well as the high theatre performances, and invariably have exciting, broad, *varied* publicity schemes. You do not have to get on a special mailing list to know what is playing at Mr. Condon's theatre – when you visit Norwich you are likely to get a leaflet from a garage forecourt, a special ticket offer delivered with your milk, to find promotional material in your magazine and to see colourful and varied advertising on every street corner. The theatre needs that populist approach. It is in contrast to many theatres and arts centres which are forbidding in appearance, demand a high reading age even to comprehend their pro-

excellent.

expenditure

motional material, and which make it plain that they are really catering for an exclusive coterie.

In seeking to make our theatres welcoming, busy places, we have perhaps gone too far in diffusing their central purpose. There are touring groups which seek to play in "found" spaces – in factories, in the streets and working men's clubs. That is fine, part of a long tradition of barnstorming theatre. Yet our theatres, which have no such aim, have often seemed to try to disguise the fact that they are theatres, existing ultimately for putting on plays in the best possible conditions. Instead, they masquerade as restaurants, shopping centres, bookshops, bars, citizens' advice bureaux, art galleries, coffee houses, rest rooms, community centres and so on – the real excitement is thus to be found in the foyers. Indeed, there are times when you can almost feel the relief at the interval, when the audience gushes forth with a sense of "Thank heavens *that's* over, now we can get down to the real social purposes of the evening..." We need to reassess not just the immediate cost of manning all those peripheral activities, but also the long-term distraction they sometimes are, for theatre staff and audience, from the central business. We should notice with irony the notice currently outside the theatre in a large and elegant English town. "Theatre open as usual", it says. (So it is – all except for the auditorium, which is being restructured. Why say "as usual"? Have they decided not to bother with plays any more?)

All this amounts to saying that we must try to put the emphasis back on the excitement of the stage. We must steer away from the pressures of the subsidising bureaucrats, who must by their natures always mistrust the popular theatre, and steer away from the modish fallacies about theatre construction and equipment. The archetypal contemporary theatre – 600 seats, expensively over-equipped, surrounded by every eating, drinking and shopping service – is fashioned in the theory that the theatre must be run by social scientists and subsidisers. It is built for a minority, built to be expensive – and, unfortunately, also built so that a great deal of the popular and even commercial drama cannot be played in it. One might even go further and say that these expensive places are built with an expectant eye upon the death of theatre; they are more than half conference centre already. The theatre cannot accommodate a rebirth if its buildings effectively deny access to a new, large audience.

That is, perhaps, the most important point of all, because the audience for *plays* is larger than it has ever been. The various dramas on television have audiences which are *massive* by former standards – and the coming of video and home video recording means that, huge though the figures are, we are probably underestimating just how often and in how many homes, the stories of *Coronation Street*, the Shakespeare canon, or *Starsky and Hutch* are seen. The theatre business must drop its traditional stance of snooty hostility to the media and recognise that television drama is not the enemy of the "live" theatre, nor is it complementary – it is a part of the same thing, another means of passing on the dramatic stories by which we all live. If the theatre can de-bureaucratise itself, can concentrate once more upon the central, simple excitement of the stage rather than the foyer, and can find ways of working *with* television and cinema, then there is no reason why once again a large number of our citizens should not go once more to hear those stories in our theatres.

List of Theatre Addresses

BRITISH THEATRE INSTITUTE,
30 Clareville Street,
London SW7 5AW.

THEATRES ADVISORY COUNCIL,
4-7 Great Pulteney Street,
London W1R 3DF.

THEATRICAL MANAGEMENT ASSOCIATION,
Bedford Chambers,
The Piazza,
Covent Garden,
London WC2 8HQ.

SOCIETY OF WEST END THEATRE,
Bedford Chambers,
The Piazza,
Covent Garden,
London WC2 8HQ.

NATIONAL COUNCIL OF THEATRE FOR
YOUNG PEOPLE,
British Theatre Centre,
9 Fitzroy Square,
London W1P 8AE.

IWOFTA,
Association of London's Fringe Theatres,
c/o Orange Tree Theatre,
45 Kew Road,
Richmond,
Surrey.

NATIONAL ASSOCIATION FOR DRAMA IN
EDUCATION AND CHILDREN'S THEATRE,
c/o British Theatre Centre,
9 Fitzroy Square,
London W1P 6AE.

BRITISH CHILDREN'S THEATRE ASSOCIATION,
9/10 Fitzroy Square,
London W1P 6AE.

INDEPENDANT THEATRE COUNCIL,
26 Abbey Road,
London NW8.

THEATRE WRITERS UNION,
9 Fitzroy Square,
London W1P 6AE.

WRITERS GUILD OF GREAT BRITAIN,
430 Edgware Road,
London W2.

NORTHERN PLAYWRIGHTS SOCIETY,
High Maidenway,
Featherstone,
Haltwhistle,
Northumberland.

SCOTTISH SOCIETY OF PLAYWRIGHTS,
346 Sauchiehall Street,
Glasgow G2 3JD.

THE SOCIETY OF AUTHORS,
84 Drayton Gardens,
London SW10 98D.

ENTERTAINMENT AGENTS' ASSOCIATION
LIMITED,
18 Charing Cross Road,
London WC2H 0HR.

VARIETY AND ALLIED ENTERTAINMENTS
COUNCIL OF GREAT BRITAIN,
18 Charing Cross Road,
London WC2H 0HR.

MUSICIANS UNION,
60-62 Clapham Road,
London SW9 0JJ.

EQUITY,
Actors' Union,
8 Harley Street,
London W1.

THE LITTLE THEATRE GUILD OF
GREAT BRITAIN,
19 Abbey Park Road,
Grimsby.

PERFORMING RIGHT SOCIETY,
29-33 Berners Street,
London W1P 4AA.

MECHANICAL COPYRIGHT PROTECTION
SOCIETY LTD.,
Elgar House,
380 Streatham High Road,
London SW16 6HR.

ARTS COUNCIL OF GREAT BRITAIN,
105 Piccadilly,
London W1V 0AU.

COMEDIA
RESEARCH · CONSULTANCY · PUBLISHING
9 Poland Street London W1V 3DG 01 439 2059

MEDIA AND COMMUNICATIONS
INDUSTRY PROFILE SERIES

This report is part of a series developed from Comedia's consultancy work in the field of media and communications. All the reports in the series will help you sort out the key issues affecting an industry from a confusing mass of facts and figures. Each report is 60pp approx. in an A4 format.

If you order more than four reports you will be entitled to claim a 25% discount. Just send your order with a cheque to Comedia (MR1), 9 Poland Street, London W1.

Please tick below those
you want to order

MARKET RESEARCH —
HEAD COUNTING BECOMES BIG BUSINESS☐
by Philip Kleinman

This report examines how much it costs to carry out market research, what people charge and from what activities research agencies make money. It looks at the use of new technology in survey work, the latest developments in qualitative market research and the changing use of omnibus surveys. It gives the background to controversies about how research is best carried out and provides a detailed who's who of the personalities behind the more profitable agencies.
Already published   ISBN 0 906 890 65 9   Paperback only: £15

THE PUBLISHING INDUSTRY☐
by Michele Field

This report provides an overview of how the British publishing industry has had to try to come to terms with its own past; an analysis of the internationalisation of the industry, looking at recent key takeovers of British publishing houses by foreign investors; and an examination of how recent moves to change the copyright laws will affect the basic economics of the industry.
Published in June, 1985   ISBN 0 906 890 61 6   Paperback only: £15

THE MUSIC INDUSTRY☐
by Phil Hardy

This report looks at the changing balance between the majors and the independents and has case studies which look at the issues surrounding home taping; the success of a multi-media distributor who started with juke boxes and a look at the management problems of a British-based major.
Published in September, 1985, ISBN 0 906 890 58 6   Paperback only: £20

FILM, VIDEO AND TV☐
by Graham Wade
Published in July, 1985, ISBN 0 906 890 63 2   Paperback only: £35

THE ART MARKET☐
Published early 1986, ISBN 0 906 890 59 4   Paperback only: £15

TELECOMMUNICATIONS☐
Published in 1986, ISBN 0 906 890 62 4   Paperback only: £25

THE COMPUTING INDUSTRY☐
Published in 1986, ISBN 0 906 890 64 0   Paperback only: £25

ELECTRONIC PUBLISHING☐
Published in 1986, ISBN 0 906 890 65 9   Paperback only: £20

THE PRINTING INDUSTRY☐
Published in 1986, ISBN 0 906 890 66 7   Paperback only: £20

ORDER FORM

Total: £.................

I have ordered four or more reports, so take off 25% ....   **Final Total:** ....

(Please make the cheque payable to Comedia and send it with this order form to Comedia (MR1), 9 Poland Street, London W1V 3DG.)

Name _____

Company _____

Address _____

_____

_____

COMEDIA

RESEARCH · CONSULTANCY · PUBLISHING

9 Poland Street London W1V 3DG 01 439 2059

Comedia is a marketing and market research consultancy. Our particular expertise lies in researching and marketing to arts audiences or readerships. Using a combination of direct mail marketing and market research, we offer:

TARGETED MARKETING: Coming from both direct mail marketing and research into audience segmentation, Comedia has put these two together to produce a powerful set of marketing tools. As the response results of the marketing can be carefully monitored, this provides vital market information. And the research pre-tests, and also lays the basis for, appropriately targeted marketing campaigns.

AUDIENCE RESEARCH: The key to successful marketing is knowing who your existing audience is and how that audience might be extended. Putting together survey work and qualitative, in-depth research, we can identify ways of enlarging your audience and where you should be directing your marketing to make this happen.

MARKETING TRAINING: Comedia runs training courses on the whole area of publicity and marketing for the arts at varying levels of sophistication. It can also offer in-house training where appropriate. This training work covers the problems of multi-event venues, touring companies, subscription schemes and many other areas. The aim is to provide ways of making scarce resources work hard.

LEISURE FUTURES: Beyond the marketing and market research work, Comedia also conducts long-term consultancy projects and has recently completed a study on the changing patterns of leisure consumption across different media for one of the major investment institutions in the public sector to identify market opportunities in multi-media retailing and distribution. The changing attitudes of users to their leisure services and the transformed patterns of public and private sector leisure consumption have clear implications for local government authorities running anything from theatres to libraries, and swimming pools to concert venues.

For further information contact David Morley at Comedia on 01-439 2059.